THE
ACCOUNTABLE
MAN

PURSUING INTEGRITY
THROUGH TRUST
AND FRIENDSHIP

TOM EISENMAN

IVP Books

An imprint of InterVarsity Press
Downers Grove, Illinois

InterVarsity Press
P.O. Box 1400, Downers Grove, IL 60515-1426
World Wide Web: www.ivpress.com
E-mail: mail@ivpress.com

InterVarsity Press® is the book-publishing division of InterVarsity Christian Fellowship/USA®, a student movement active on campus at hundreds of universities, colleges and schools of nursing in the United States of America, and a member movement of the International Fellowship of Evangelical Students. For information about local and regional activities, write Public Relations Dept., InterVarsity Christian Fellowship/USA, 6400 Schroeder Rd., P.O. Box 7895, Madison, WI 53707-7895, or visit the IVCF website at <www.intervarsity.org>.

Cover design: Cindy Kiple
Cover image: David Sacks/Getty Images

ISBN-10: 0-8308-2382-4
ISBN-13: 978-0-8308-2382-6

Printed in the United States of America ∞

Library of Congress Cataloging-in-Publication Data

Eisenman, Tom.
   The accountable man: pursuing integrity through trust and friendship
   / Tom Eisenman.
     p. cm.
   ISBN 0-8308-2382-4 (pbk.: alk. paper)
   1. Christian men—religious life. 2. Male friendship—religious
aspects—Christianity. I. Title.
   BV4528.2.E445 2003
   241'.6762'081·dc21

                                                   2002156375

P	16	15	14	13	12	11	10	9	8
Y	17	16	15	14	13	12			

I dedicate this book to the men who have been my true guides and spiritual companions through the years, especially Dean Uhls, James Croegaert, Paul Annett, Tim Grice, Tom Miller, Jim Fletemeyer, Dave Lee, Dick Tumpes, Tom Zimmerman, Bruce Juhlin, Peter Hiett, Jim Osterhaus, Chuck Harris, Ken Strong, Eric Johnson, Cal Saunders, Jim Rohrer, Ron Barrett, Ernst Mikkelson, Dave Bowman, Jeffrey Long, Pat Parlin, Jack Finley, Jason, Josh, Gabe, and all the other men today who have caught the vision and are passionate about challenging one another to live each day in the love and holiness of Christ.

CONTENTS

1 THE ACCOUNTABLE MAN

BILL AND LARRY SAT DOWN FOR LUNCH at a corner table in the local coffee shop. After ordering, there was a moment of awkward silence. Then Larry opened the conversation. "Bill, I wanted to get together with you today because I feel I'm missing out on something in life."

Surprised, Bill chuckled and said, "You, Larry? You've got to be kidding."

"Why?" Larry asked, perplexed.

"Because it seems like you've got it all together. Great marriage and family, super job, solid Christian faith. I've often wished I could be more like you. What could be missing from your life?"

"Well, what's missing is . . ." Larry paused and looked away for a moment before finishing, "I really don't have any close friends."

Bill sat quietly for a second or two. "You really mean that, don't you?"

"Yeah. That's why I asked you to lunch today. To talk about that."

"Well, okay. But why me?"

"Because we've worked together on some things at

church," Larry replied, "and we've talked some at soccer
with the kids. I guess I would just say I like you and would
like to know if we could meet on some regular basis. I'd like
to see if there's a friendship waiting to happen here."

After another short pause, Larry continued, "I feel kind of
embarrassed admitting I don't have any friends. I also feel
funny just coming out and asking you like this. But I don't
know how else to start a friendship."

Bill took a sip of his coffee before answering. "You know,
Larry, there are a lot of people who would want to be friends
with you."

"There are?" Larry acted surprised. "Nobody ever calls
me or asks me to do anything."

"Well, maybe that's because you send out some pretty
strong signals about how busy you are. You're always talking about how many things you're juggling, that you travel
so much you don't even have time for your own family.
Who's going to ask you to do something more?"

"I guess you're right." Larry smiled, "But see, this is what
I've always liked about you, even in our brief talks. You're one
of the few men I know who will tell me the truth. I know that's
what's missing in my life. I'm looking for a friend who cares
enough to be honest and tell me what I need to hear."

"Well, I'd like that kind of friendship too," Bill said, looking straight at Larry. "But it would have to be mutual. I have
a lot of the same needs you do. And I'd also like to kick back
sometimes and just have fun, if we decide to spend more time
together. Would you be up for that?"

"Sure. My life has a way of getting way too serious. Sometimes I feel like I'm going to break. I need some fun in my life."

Bill put down his coffee mug and said, "I think we should pray about this for a few days, then get back together and see where the Lord leads. We should check with our families about this too, because of the time commitment. Good friendships take time and attention."

"I think I just realized that if I'm too busy to have friends, I'm too busy. I'm not going to live like that anymore," Larry declared. "But I need help too, to change my old habits."

"I think we might be a great help to each other," Bill said. "I'm excited to see what God's going to do here."

It was well over a decade ago that I learned one of the truest, most important and lasting lessons ever about how to live a lifestyle of continued renewal in Jesus.

I had been drifting for about two years in a period I would now describe as the doldrums of a self-satisfied Christian life. A ship that is in the doldrums has entered into a region where the wind has died. There is no surge of energy to power the ship forward and keep it on course. Light and shifting winds put the ship into a pattern of directionless meandering.

That's how I would describe that former period of my Christian life—directionless meandering. The greatest danger in it was how comfortable I had begun to feel in that place. I know now how lifeless my Christianity had become, but back then things seemed to be going pretty well for me in my family, my job, my relationships and—yes—even my "religious" life.

It's easy to settle for something less, even when we know deep down that God wants us to experience the very best. When comforts and worldly distractions obscure the larger vision in our lives, we're good at rationalizing our present state of affairs. Rationalizations are a wonderful help in making us feel fine about our life when in reality many things may be on the slide.

What brought the situation to a head for me was signing a contract with my publisher to do a book called *Temptations Men Face*. I received an advance (which I quickly spent) and then went several months without being able to write a word. Things got tense. I finally took a morning off work and stayed home for the purpose of getting to the bottom of this with God. I sat on our back deck in the sun and prayed fervently. I was crying out to God to do something to break through my severe case of writer's block. I was convinced that my inability to work on this project was an attack of the evil one. But somewhere during that extended time of prayer I began getting a faint sense that God might not be swallowing my line of reasoning. At one point I stopped to take a breath, and God started talking to me.

Before long, I had written down on my note pad a number of areas in my life that God was putting his finger on. He was basically saying to me that morning that he would not bless my writing project on temptation while I was ignoring areas in my life where my behaviors and attitudes were less than pleasing to him. He was showing me that my refusal to deal with these sin areas was hurting my relationship with him, standing in the way of my personal growth and blessing, and keeping me from moving forward in ministry and service to him. Writing a book on resisting temptation while I was in denial in some important areas of integrity was a hypocrisy God refused to bless.

I repented on my knees. I experienced in my heart what Paul meant when he said, "Godly sorrow brings repentance that leads to salvation [or for me, deliverance] and leaves no regret" (2 Cor 7:10). God led me then to make a covenant with him regarding the things that were listed on my pad. I could sense the energy of the Holy Spirit working in me. It felt like light and life. The excitement was motivating and empowering. But almost immediately I realized that God wanted me to take another step. As doubts crept in, and as I sensed that I would soon face some strong temptations to settle again for life in the doldrums, even to return to sin, I knew God wanted me to take a further step to help make this renewal experience lasting.

It was clear what God wanted me to do. The next

morning I was meeting with my small group of men; it was my opportunity to bring my areas of struggle into the light and ask for the prayer and support of these men who loved me. I shared the experience of the previous morning and asked my close friends to hold me accountable to the covenant I had made with God. They agreed to pray for me and ask me regularly how I was doing. I knew I could count on their love and support, and I knew they were the kind of men who would challenge me without judging or dismissing me.

That was the day I learned the power of accountable relationships to help a man deepen his walk with God. I have never been the same since that day when I risked opening my life more fully to those men. I learned that day, and in the months and years to come, what Christian friendship is really all about and how God intends to use trusted relationships to purify our character and continually transform and revitalize our relationship with him. Within days of that small group meeting, my writer's block was gone and I was well into the book.

The lesson I learned can be stated in this principle: *Renewal begins in repentance and continues in obedience, strengthened by accountability.* God had to lead me to the place where I saw my sin for what it was and felt true sorrow over it. He also led me into repentance, which means turning away from the sin and toward obedience, depending on the power of God for life change. The final step was a step into the light where I shared my good intentions with others whose love, support and prayer would help me stand firm. That is how we begin to live the accountable life.

ACCOUNTABILITY IS NOT FOR SISSIES

As we mature in Christ, we at some point realize that a significant change is taking place in us. We are developing a hunger to feed others in the way we ourselves have been nourished, to make a difference in the lives of those around us for Jesus' sake. The experience is both an awakening and a deepening that occur supernaturally as Christ is formed in us (Gal 4:19). Early in our Christian lives it is all about us—what God is doing for us, the blessings we are receiving. But now, more and more, we want it all to be for him.

This shift in the tectonic plates of our spiritual nature changes the entire landscape of our lives. The emerging vision brings a revitalized life in Christ. But along with the excitement of this new season of life come new and weighty challenges.

We see more clearly what we with all our heart want to become. And we see just as clearly how much we still need to grow in order to be everything we hope to be for the Lord. The new challenges at this stage can seem overwhelming. Doubts flood in. How will we stay the course and overcome all those unhealthy habits that have held us back in the past? Who will help us discern which of God's great promises is most applicable to our present season of life? How will we evaluate with any confidence whether we are making progress with God? To whom can we turn for confirmation of

God's call for our lives? Who will stand with us in the battle when the going gets rough?

Of course, the Lord is our strength and guide in all these matters. But in his wisdom, he has also given us the gift of brothers in the body of Christ. Brothers in Christ will walk with us and stand by us, and they can become wonderful spiritual friends to bring the guidance of God's Word to us while supporting us in prayer.

Life in God is not just about God and me alone. God's design for Christian living is about God and me and others. The Christian life needs both vertical and horizontal love relationships in order to be complete. It is loving God with all my heart and loving my neighbor as myself. "For we were all baptized by one Spirit into one body" (1 Cor 12:13). We are made for each other in the body of Christ.

In Ephesians 3:14-19 the apostle Paul describes God's design for life in the Christian community. In this passage Paul says that God is our Father and that all of us who believe are members of his eternal family. He prays for us to grasp "together" the true nature of God's amazing unconditional love. This love is the source for everything we do in our Christian lives. As Christian men, our main task in life is to learn better how to both receive God's love and extend God's love to others.

To learn to love as God loves is the essence of our call. And living in intimate relationship with others who claim Christ as Savior is the school that God determined would best develop in us this kind of mature, self-sacrificial living. To learn to love as Jesus loves is our path toward mature manhood. Beautifully, God intends us to enjoy both the challenge and the encouragement that come from being deeply engaged with other growing men in Christian community.

WHAT IS ACCOUNTABILITY, AND WHY DO WE NEED IT?

In essence, the accountable man is a Christian man who is willing to risk opening his life to others in order to become answerable for his attitudes and actions. In this book I will be suggesting that it is essential for us to have at least one friend we can count on to speak the truth to us in love (Eph 4:15). The Word of God is truth to guide our lives. But our human nature, which the Bible calls our "flesh," is at war with God (Rom 8:7-12). That is why we need other spiritual men to help us see where there is inconsistency between what we say we believe and how we actually live. It takes great maturity for a man to risk entering into this kind of honest relationship. When you are ready to take this step, you are stating your serious commitment to be everything you can be for Christ.

As we grow in Christ and in relationship with others who love us, we will grow in our ability to trust God and to trust close Christian friends. We can overcome our fear of disclosure. And as we learn to take risks in relationship, our circle of accountability will expand. We will find that we are giving to an increasing number of men the right to examine us, to question, to give counsel, to pray with us, to share life with us at the deeper levels. The greater our influence of leader-

ship, the broader should be our circle of accountable relationships. If we are serious about developing godly
character, we will choose to be in healthy, mutual relationships with others, learning better how to live and
work in partnership.

If we desire to develop mature Christian character,
we will quickly realize that we need this strength, insight and support. If we are really listening, wisdom
from above will reveal to us early on that we have an
innate sinful tendency to excuse ourselves, rationalize
our behavior or just plain live in denial. We rationalize
when we come up with creative excuses to cover up
our sin. Denial is blindness, our inability to even see
the sinfulness in many of our choices.

Scripture teaches that if we are left to our own de-
vices, we are hopelessly lost. We will only deceive ourselves and try to deceive others if we can. The truth
about our natural inclinations is captured in the following Scripture verses:

> The heart is deceitful above all things
>   and beyond cure.
>   Who can understand it? (Jer 17:9)

> The LORD saw how great man's wickedness on
> the earth had become, and that every inclina-
> tion of the thoughts of his heart was only evil all
> the time. (Gen 6:5)

> He who trusts in himself is a fool,
>   but he who walks in wisdom is kept safe.
> (Prov 28:26)

A Christian man who gladly enters into relationships that provide regular face-to-face encounters with other men is a man who walks in wisdom. We need to lovingly get in each other's faces to help break down our natural tendencies toward conducting secret lives or living in constant rationalization and denial. We all need good friends in the Lord who can reflect the truth to us in such a way that we will be able to see clearly when we are just playing games with God.

CHOOSING ACCOUNTABILITY

Choosing to become accountable to others takes real courage. There are risks in the relationship. Accountability will not work unless there is real honesty and vulnerability between the men regarding their struggles and shortfalls. The relationship requires a commitment of time, too, as the men involved take on the challenge of praying for one another and meeting regularly enough to be an encouragement to each other. A man in an accountable relationship will have to be learning more each day how to confront in love and to challenge his brothers without bringing unnecessary judgment. The most beneficial context in which men can encourage one another to be everything they can be in God is always a nonjudgmental environment of unconditional love, forgiveness and encouragement.

The concept of accountability is rooted in Scripture. The following are just a few verses that suggest the importance of developing accountable relationships.

Wounds from a friend can be trusted,
　　but an enemy multiplies kisses. (Prov 27:6)

Pride only breeds quarrels,
　　but wisdom is found in those who take advice.
(Prov 13:10)

He who ignores discipline comes to poverty
　　　and shame,
　　but whoever heeds correction is honored.
(Prov 13:18)

As iron sharpens iron,
　　so one man sharpens another. (Prov 27:17)

Not to be shaped by the Word is to be shaped by the world (Rom 12:2). I believe there is a new call from God to Christian men today to enter wholeheartedly into this costly battle for integrity. Strength for fighting the good fight over the long haul comes from learning to stand arm in arm and heart to heart with other men.

Forming growing and lasting friendships does not come naturally for many men. But we can learn to develop quality mutual relationships. We can learn to become mutual mentors and spiritual directors for one another. We can learn the skills to be better encouragers, sincere forgivers, holy listeners, unconditional lovers, wise counselors, spiritual guides, bold challengers, Christlike leaders.

Every Christian man has the potential to be a strong leader, a man of influence for Christ in his world. But effective kingdom leadership requires a willingness to submit our lives to Christ on a daily basis and to submit ourselves to the godly leadership of other men.

FOR REFLECTION OR DISCUSSION

1. List reasons why being in an accountable relationship can strengthen your walk with God.

2. Why do you think the author says, "The greater our influence of leadership, the broader should be our circle of accountable relationships"?

3. This chapter says that the tough work of holding one another accountable happens best in a nonjudgmental environment of unconditional love. Explain in your own words what you think this kind of relational environment looks like.

4. Which of the Scripture passages mentioned in this chapter are particularly meaningful to you and why?

2

WHEN TWO ARE BETTER THAN ONE

BILL AND LARRY MET AGAIN *the middle of the next week. They decided to get together early, before work, at a pancake house a few blocks from Bill's place.*

"Larry, I've been thinking and praying a lot about this all week," Bill said.

"Me too. What do you think?" Larry asked a little hesitantly.

"I think the Lord is putting this together," Bill said with a smile.

"Man, I'm glad to hear you say that. I've been feeling good about it too. So I was really looking forward to this morning. Then I was afraid you might turn me down."

"Funny," Bill responded. "I was afraid of that too. That's probably why a lot of guys don't reach out in friendship: fear of rejection. So we just keep doing our own thing."

"Yeah, doing it all alone," Larry reflected. "That's how I've felt for a long time too."

"What's that?"

"Alone. And I don't want that anymore. This week I was

reading in Ecclesiastes where it talks about two being better than one. If one falls down, his friend can help him up. And then it said something like, 'But pity the man who falls and has no one to help him up!' "

"That's a favorite of mine," Bill said, taking a bite of his waffle.

"Well, it had never hit me before. And it seemed like a word from the Lord on the importance of friendship. It felt like confirmation from God to make it a priority to develop at least one good friendship with a brother in Christ."

"I have a real sense of God's leading in this," Bill said. "What seemed to become clear to me as I prayed was that we should probably first just get to know each other better. I know we both want to hold each other accountable in our walk, but I think that kind of trust can grow best if we work first on our friendship."

"I like that. How about just doing something for fun together each month? Just the two of us. Something to enjoy and help us get to know each other better." Larry's eyes lit up. "I get sports tickets through my work, and we can go to some games together."

"I'd like that. Or catch a movie together—you know, the movies you and I would like but Karen and Diane would never go to see with us!"

Both men laughed.

Bill continued, "Or play some tennis. Or we could go to that new pool place and shoot a few games."

"That would be fun," Larry agreed. "I haven't played

pool in years! We should try to get our families together too."

"Sounds like a plan. And if this is a good time for us to meet each week, we can work on what to do with this time—what to study, maybe, and what we would both like to get out of this personal time together."

"I'm fine with that. At the very least, we can start by praying for each other. Bill, how can I pray for you?"

Bill started with a few prayer requests about work and family. Larry followed suit and then suggested praying for their friendship to deepen and grow. They were off and running.

The men who have been friends and partners with me along the way have enriched my life beyond measure. I am in complete agreement with King Solomon about the value of good friends. He said:

> Two are better than one,
>   because they have a good return for their
>   work:
> If one falls down,
>   his friend can help him up.
> But pity the man who falls
>   and has no one to help him up!

Also, if two lie down together, they will
   keep warm.
But how can one keep warm alone?
Though one may be overpowered,
   two can defend themselves.
A cord of three strands is not quickly broken.
(Eccles 4:9-12)

This biblical passage states clearly the benefits of walking in partnership with others. It touches on the topics of fruitfulness and productivity in shared life and ministry. Tremendous blessings come to us from relationships of mutual support and encouragement. We experience greater strength when we stand together with others and hold a common goal, vision and commitment.

Solomon said the friendless person is to be pitied. The person who tries to go it alone is missing out. Blessed are we if we have someone there to lift us up when we're down, to comfort us, pray for us and share godly wisdom when we feel lonely or afraid, hurt or mistreated. Blessed are we if we have friends who will stand with us when we are attacked, whether the attacks come from other people or from the evil one. There is nothing better than to have friends who will defend us, bringing strength in numbers to fight the good fight.

Blessed are we, too, when we find that God has brought another person into our lives to help us be more productive. Through the blending of unique gifts and personalities, my friend and I contribute something to the kingdom of God together that would never have come into being without our partnership. The Scripture passage above teaches that if we work in cooperation with a good partner, we will enjoy a better return for the effort we put in. These are just some of the joys and blessings that result from having close godly friends.

THE STAGES OF MATURING FRIENDSHIPS

Good relationships in the Lord have a natural progression, passing through certain stages.

First comes the simple enjoyment of spending time with someone you like. There is a chemistry to a good friendship. You will generally recognize early in a relationship whether the liking is reciprocal, whether both of you respect and appreciate each other, and whether you can relate easily.

The second stage is the deepening of the relationship through trust. You find that the other person cares about what happens in your life, and you begin caring more about him. You enjoy talking together about all the areas of common interest you might have—sports and work, family and recreation—but you find yourself increasingly able to talk about deeper things in life as well. Trust develops in the relationship because you are both sincere in expressions of help and support, and you demonstrate to one another that you can be trusted to hold in confidence the more sensitive issues. Christian men who want to develop their good friendships also go deeper by praying for and with each other and sharing biblical insights. Greater honesty and intimacy enter into the relationship at this stage.

A third stage in the maturing of a relationship is growing accountability. If we really care about the other person, we will take the risk to suggest that our good friend may be getting off track in his priorities or using poor judgment. We may even tell him that we see a pattern of sin and rationalization developing in his life. We take an active interest in encouraging the very best in one another in our family lives, our work lives, our spiritual lives, our ministry pursuits. Good Christian friends take seriously the challenge from Hebrews 10:24: "Let us consider how we may spur one another on toward love and good deeds."

Friends reach a rewarding final stage when they sense a call from God on their lives and respond by serving him faithfully together in some capacity in the church or in the world. This service grows the relationship because you realize that God has put you together with another person to achieve something that reaches beyond personal growth toward meeting the needs of others. God has fitted your friendship with a unique blend of gifts that allows you to accomplish something together that neither of you could have managed alone. You feel great pleasure in being part of a work God is accomplishing as a direct result of a friendship cemented by love, mutual respect and a deep commitment to the Lord.

ONE STORY OF GROWING FRIENDSHIPS

A group of friends I enjoyed in Colorado offers a prime example of how this kind of partnership develops in the Lord.

I was new on the staff of a large church in Boulder and was eager to find a new friend. I had left some close friends behind in Minnesota, and I was feeling the loss. When you've had quality friendships with other men, it's hard to move to a new place and start all over again. So I was happy when a small group of men in the church invited me to join them.

This group turned out to be one of the greatest blessings in my life. My involvement with these men lasted nearly ten years. The key members stayed together the whole time, while other men would come in for a season and then move on.

At first there occurred the testing of relationships that always takes place as men get to know one another. In a small group it is typically true that you will grow closer to one man, or a few of the men, than you will to others. The potential to develop a deep and lasting friendship in the Lord is not there in every relationship.

Just because you don't relate as easily with a certain man doesn't mean that man won't be valuable to you as a Christian brother. We need Christian friends who do not always agree with us or see everything the way we do. Having to contend with differences of opinion or approach is valuable for us in developing a broader perspective and in learning to love others who are not like us. We need to welcome differences in personality, giftedness and perspective.

Still, it is best for us to spend most of our relational time with one man or a couple of men with whom we really hit it off. One important sign at the beginning of something good is being able to have fun in our Christian friendship with another man. In my Colorado group, we did have fun.

One time a member of our group was getting married and the rest of us wanted to do something special for his wedding. We decided to go dressed as Musketeers. We rented ruffled white shirts, swords, Musketeer hats—the whole thing. On the day of the wedding we sat in the back of the church. When the groom took his place up front and turned to face the people, he saw us in back and shook his head in disbelief. After the pronouncement, the bride and groom headed up the aisle. We stood on both sides, rapiers raised, blades touching at the top, as the new couple headed out between us. People at the reception wanted to know who the groom's Musketeer friends were. "The guys from my Bible study," he told them. We have laughed together about that memory for years.

One of the best things about having a friendship with another man or a small group of men is doing things together that men like to do. We would grab time whenever we could to play volleyball in the park or take in a sporting event. We had men's nights out to play pool, go bowling or see an action movie our wives wouldn't have enjoyed. Afterward we'd get a hamburger or a dessert and just sit and talk, catching up on each other's families, sharing our lives.

We also enjoyed getting together as families. Some of our children are still best friends, and our wives stay in contact with each other to this day even though many of us have moved away. It is great to have friends you can kick back with and really be yourself, without having to project an image or be deadly serious all the time.

GOING DEEPER

In my Colorado small group, we enjoyed our friendships, but that wasn't the whole of what our relationship was about. From that initial stage of getting to know one another, we grew closer by praying for one another and meeting in a weekly Bible study. Differences often emerged—differences in lifestyle, in theology, in opinions on what makes a good marriage and family. It was a refreshingly honest experience to get beneath the surface politeness of the honeymoon stage of relationships to the real issues of each other's lives. Learning to respect our differences while accepting one another, and choosing to continue in love, created the possibility for authentic friendships that grew in vulnerability and honesty.

We also lived through many hard times together. One man in the group might have been going through job insecurity and financial stresses, while another had a child who required risky surgery. One man might have been going through depression, while another man couldn't find time to work on his marriage. It is no small thing to have someone you can go to when life turns sour.

We shared many victories and joys as well. There were births, home purchases, children's successes in school or sports, job promotions. Just as important as having someone to go to when times are tough is having a friend who is eager to share in your excitement when you're on the mountaintop. Having a Christian friend gives one an opportunity to "rejoice with those who rejoice; mourn with those who mourn" (Rom 12:15).

STEPPING IT UP: ACCOUNTABILITY

It was a natural step in our spiritual journey together that we began developing deeper, more accountable relationships with one another. If you risk sharing honestly with other men, and if you are accepted and supported by them, your trust level grows. It always amazes me how quickly men can get over the fear of appearing foolish.

Accountability in the form of mutual encouragement and challenge grew in that small group during the whole time I participated in it. And I know that meaningful accountability occurred one-on-one between men outside of our group meetings as well. Some situations in a man's life can be so personal that it would be difficult, if not inappropriate, to bring it to the group time. We were all friends, but with issues requiring the greatest confidentiality, one man in the group might seek out one other man with whom he felt a stronger chemistry or comfort. That's how it worked for us.

This is a book on accountability, but I would like to emphasize here that I believe a friendship in Christ develops first. Accountability is really a secondary re-

sult of a deepening friendship. You aim at a friendship and you develop the relationship. As you grow
in appreciation of each other as friends, and as you
trust each other more, it becomes a natural step to begin holding one another accountable in matters of the
Christian walk.

This kind of trust can occur fairly early in a relationship if you are making the friendship a priority in your
life. But without trust, accountability can't happen.
You have to trust your friend—know that he has your
best interests in mind—before you will be comfortable
sharing how you have struggled with a pattern of repeated sin in your life. In fact, you need a level of trust
before you can even share about something less personal, such as not really knowing how to pray. It takes
mutual trust before you will risk confronting your
friend about the fact that he seldom encourages his
wife or children. It takes mutual trust for him to listen
and let you help him begin to practice this new communication style in the family.

Accountability is also supporting one another in
the basic disciplines of the Christian faith—prayer, Bible study, worship, service. It is encouraging one another to live out biblical principles in every area of our
lives—in our families, our businesses and our friendships. It is being willing to remind each other when
our conversation is slipping into gossip or we are taking on a critical or sarcastic attitude. Accountability is
listening for a word from God for our brother and then
encouraging him with that word. I will talk much

more about accountability, how it works and the skills we need to be good accountability partners in the chapters that follow.

SERVING GOD TOGETHER

As I have already mentioned, one delight in a good Christian friendship comes when we serve God together. We create something together that God can use for good, and it is something that would never have come into being if our friendship had not existed. It is the unique blend of two or more persons and personalities, with their complementary gifts, that creates the possibility for a specific ministry to arise.

There came a time in my service in that church in Colorado when I was asked if I would take on the development of a new ministry to university students. As soon as I was approached with the idea, I thought of my friends in the men's Bible study group. I have always believed that a ministry team should really *be* the church to one another before they try to *do the work* of the church. The most effective ministry teams are those that are involved first in serving each other through support, accountability and prayer before they try to serve the larger body of Christ or the world. The quality of our relationships in a ministry team—whether it's two men or ten—will determine the quality of the ministry that is accomplished. Our mutual care and accountability is that important to the success of our service in the Lord.

The next time we were together, I approached the

men's group with the idea of teaming up to take this risk of ministry together. I talked about the fact that if I were to gather another group to work with, it would take a year or more to get those new relationships to the point where we could work freely and effectively together. In contrast, the Bible study guys had been together for several years. So we had a good understanding of what our mix of gifts and personalities would bring to this ministry to students if we were to step up and do it together. We knew at the onset which of the men would be best at pulling off the social events, who would work well together to plan the retreats, who had the gifts for leading Bible studies. We knew which couples would be excellent counselors for kids in trouble and which ones in the group were wild and crazy enough to be up-front leaders at the student gatherings.

Furthermore, we already knew that everything we did together—the fun times and the growth times—was enjoyable; all of it added to the richness of our lives. This would be just another step together with God that promised the excitement of going on to new levels of relationship. We really did have a sense that we had been called by God into relationship together—but not just to be friends to grow each other and support each other. We believed there was a larger purpose behind God's choice to put us together at that place and at that time.

Nobody in the group could say no to this challenge. Ephesians 2:10 applied directly to our situation: "We are God's workmanship, created in Christ Jesus to do good works, which God prepared in advance for us to do." We believed that our meeting and becoming friends and partners was no accident. God had created our ministry team in Christ Jesus and had prepared in advance a good work for us to do together. God had already taken us through so much together; we had confidence that he would step with us into this new dimension of living out our call. We were all eager to get started.

The two years we devoted to student ministry was another chapter in the story of God's blessing on our friendship. We enjoyed even deeper growth together, continuing accountability in our personal lives and ministry, and the added blessing of seeing God produce something that was greater than any of us as individuals. We could celebrate God's work with us as a divinely appointed partnership. What a joy!

CHOOSING FRIENDSHIP

My hope is that if you didn't appreciate before the joy and help that can come from a friendship with another man, I have whet your appetite. Many men have an independent spirit and think they are better off doing it all on their own. But the opening Scripture from Ecclesiastes alone ought to be enough to convince you that God wants you to be in relationship with others. It is his design for effective living. Men who want to grow in Christ will be eager to find and develop at least one good friendship with another godly man.

The next chapter will help you think through how

important it is to choose the right kind of friend to walk
closely with in the Lord.

FOR REFLECTION OR DISCUSSION

1. List the benefits you have received from good
   friends.

2. Summarize in your own words what the author describes as the natural progression of friendships. Tell
   why you agree or disagree with this analysis.

3. In this chapter the author states, "God has fitted
   your friendship with a unique blend of gifts that allows you to accomplish something together that neither of you could have managed alone." How have
   you seen that to be true?

4. Write below how you believe a good accountability
   friendship would enrich your Christian life.

5. Why does it make sense that men who have walked
   closely in their personal lives would make strong
   ministry teams? List all the reasons that come to
   mind.

3   WHAT TO LOOK FOR IN
       A CHRISTIAN FRIEND

"THIS IS GOING PRETTY GOOD, HUH?" Larry said as he spread orange marmalade on his bagel.

"Sure is," Bill replied. "And thanks for having us over last weekend. The barbecue was great. Karen and Diane really seemed to hit it off too."

"And the kids had a great time together."

"I know mine did. They talked about Nick and Angie all the way home."

Bill took a couple of sips of his steaming coffee, then he gave the conversation a more serious turn. "Larry, can I say something that's on my mind?"

"Sure. That's why we're meeting, right?"

"Well, as we get to know each other better, I hope you won't be disappointed that I have some real areas of struggle in my life." Bill paused again. "I am going to need your help to grow in my obedience in some of these areas."

"I'm not sure why you're worried about that," Larry replied. "We've all got things we need help in."

"Well, you didn't really say this in so many words before,

but I got the feeling that you might have seen me as someone who has it all together spiritually. So I just wanted to make sure you heard me when I said this would have to be a mutual relationship. I struggle with some real issues. And I wondered if you'd still take me seriously if you knew that I really, really need accountability and support myself."

"Bill, if I've picked up anything from you so far, it's that you have a real heart for God. I know you really want to grow in the Lord."

"Yes, I do," Bill affirmed. "And I know you do too."

"But neither of us is perfect," Larry pointed out. "If one of us was already perfected in the Lord, there would be no point in meeting like this, right?"

"No, there wouldn't. It's all about making progress in our relationship with God. Not about being perfect, but about staying in the fight."

"Exactly." Larry became more animated. "If you acted like you had it all together, I wouldn't get anything out of meeting with you. You show a real willingness to be honest with me about what you see in me, and it seems like you're just as eager to listen to me if I have to confront you about something. That's something I admire about you. I don't see you as a guy who plays games with God or who is trying to put on some false front with me. That's refreshing. I want to be the same way with you."

Bill nodded. "I guess if this is really going to work we both need to trust that God has put us together in this relationship. He knows we will be good for each other. We'll just have to keep working on being as honest as we can in sharing things, even those dark places in our lives."

"I think God works when we bring some of those things out into the open. That verse in James says we should confess our sins to one another so that we may be healed." Larry grinned. "I'm just glad I'm not the only one here who has things to confess."

Both men laughed, relieved.

"Well, I just wanted to get that clear," Bill said. "I was hoping you weren't expecting me to be some kind of guru with all the answers. I'm not perfect, you know. But I do care about my walk with God. And I look forward to our friendship working for both of us, to bring out the best that we can be."

"It's not about perfect performance. It's about helping each other make progress."

"That's real wisdom," Bill chuckled. "Now I suppose I have to pick up the check!"

We all need accountability if we are to grow in Christ. I would like to emphasize again, though, that a good and lasting accountability relationship generally develops out of a quality friendship in Christ. What we are really looking for first is a friend. And then, if we sense the relationship is working, that may be a sign that God is trying to put an accountability arrangement together.

A lot is at stake in an accountability relationship. It is important for us to take time to make a godly decision about who to go deeper with. Not every Christian man will be right for us as a friend and accountability partner. We can make mistakes, and if we're not wise, it is easy to get wounded.

I remember one man who wanted to develop an accountability relationship with me. He talked about what he saw in me that gave him hope that we could have a deeper friendship. I was open to it. We met regularly for a time, and I kept asking God whether I should continue to develop this accountable friendship.

I tried hard, but something kept me from opening up. At one point, finally, I told the man that I would be happy to meet with him as his pastor and counsel and pray with him, but that I didn't feel free to enter into a mutual relationship at that time. He was disappointed, but he continued to meet with me for a while and share some needs with me. Our relationship was not mutual.

Some time after that we came to have a difference of opinion about our vision for the church. The man came to me and attempted to use the influence of our relationship to sway things his way. When he couldn't enlist me in his private cause, our friendship suddenly came to an end.

The man was influential in the church, and we went through a period of struggle over the issues of change. Many times during that difficult period I thanked the Lord for protecting me from becoming more vulnerable and disclosing more of my private life to the man.

This is why it is so important to pursue godly wisdom with much prayer in seeking a friend to become a long-term accountability partner. You may ask, "With so much at stake, why should I take the risk?" It is worth the risk because your continued growth in the Lord depends on it. To know that there is someone you can call on day or night when you need a friend is a gift from God. To have a person with whom you can be yourself and be accepted and loved—that is what's really at stake. Fear of disclosure can rob us of one of the best gifts available to us in the church: trusted friendships with others. We take this step cautiously and wisely, with discernment, but we take the step.

Stop and think for a moment. Have you experienced any significant life change that has not come through a relationship you've had with a person you trusted? Have you learned and retained any insight that has not come through a relationship? That's how important quality friendships are to our growth as Christian men. And that's why it is imperative that we surround ourselves with the right kind of people. Proverbs 13:20 says, "He who walks with the wise grows wise, but a companion of fools suffers harm."

It is important to grasp this principle. Those we choose to enter into relationship with will affect our lives. They will impact our thinking and our actions. Our spiritual lives will be influenced in one direction or another based on the company we keep. Thus our choices about the relationships we enter into are among the most critical we will make in our lives.

ENLISTING FRIENDS FOR SPIRITUAL DEVELOPMENT

If my chances of growing stronger, wiser and deeper in the Lord are enhanced by choosing people I know will be good for me, then I will make these friendship choices carefully and prayerfully. Some of the people in my circle should be there, not just because they are nice to be around, but because I have nurtured relationships with them, knowing they will be good for my growth.

If I want to grow in wisdom, I will look for men to be in my friendship team who demonstrate good judgment. If I want to grow in compassion for others, I will want friends on my team who model mercy. If I desire a deeper awareness of God, then I need to be in long-term relationships with men who are disciplined in their faith. I want people close to me who take seriously the lifestyle challenge from Hebrews 10:24: "Let us consider how we may spur one another on toward love and good deeds."

There is also a strong warning to heed in Proverbs 13:20: "A companion of fools suffers harm." I want to be just as actively engaged in steering clear of people who could lead me astray as I am in choosing to spend more time with people who are good for me.

The apostle Paul affirmed this principle by warning, "Do not be misled: 'Bad company corrupts good character' " (1 Cor 15:33). Note that Paul was not saying that the wrong kinds of friends will lead a weak and stumbling person astray. Rather, he was saying that you can be a person of "good character," that is, a strong person, but you still have to be careful about the company you keep.

In every fellowship, it seems, there are men and women who are like viruses looking for host cells. If we are not wise, we can open our lives to people who do not have a godly agenda. When we receive people like this, we become infected, and we will eventually infect others if we are not careful.

Don't be a host cell to people with destructive life patterns. Don't get sucked in to gossip or listen to slanderous remarks that are coming second- and third-hand. Don't let yourself be drawn into an unethical business deal. Don't hang around with people who live a lifestyle characterized by these kinds of questionable behaviors. Be on your guard.

It isn't that people who have destructive and sinful patterns don't matter. They do! They matter to God, and so they had better matter to us. We are to take every opportunity to help them follow Christ and to serve and love them, being patient and forgiving with them. But Paul said bad company can corrupt our good character. And Peter similarly said, "Be on your guard so that you may not be carried away by the error of lawless men and fall from your secure position" (2 Pet 3:17). So while we should minister to people like this, they are not the people we want to invite into our inner circle of friends.

BIBLICAL WARNING SIGNS

The Bible gives us clear guidance on behaviors that should raise red flags when we see them in men we are considering as close friends. Here is our guide.

> There are six things the LORD hates,
>   seven that are detestable to him:
>   haughty eyes,
>   a lying tongue,
>   hands that shed innocent blood,
>   a heart that devises wicked schemes,
>   feet that are quick to rush into evil,
>   a false witness who pours out lies
>   and a man who stirs up dissension among
>   brothers. (Prov 6:16-19)

When we pick up tendencies toward these behaviors in others, we need to be cautious. Let's not be quick to add a man to our buddy list who struggles with any of these life patterns.

"Haughty eyes" describes the person of pride who thinks he has arrived and has it all together. And sadly, it is quite common for people who have been in the church for many years to be people of pride. They reason, *I have come to a place of special discernment in the Lord, so now I can judge my brothers and sisters.* If you hang around people like this, you too will become critical and judgmental. Do not let their arrogance spill over into your life. Proverbs 16:18 says, "Pride goes before destruction, a haughty spirit before a fall."

Then there is the person with a "lying tongue." If

you enter into a friendship with a man who has trouble being honest, you are setting yourself up to be used, deceived and betrayed. If you want to be a person who can be trusted to speak the truth and fulfill the promises you make, don't hang around with people who treat the truth as if it is negotiable. Their deceptive ways will rub off on you. And it is virtually impossible to have accountability that works without the regular practice of mutual truth telling in the relationship.

The shedding of "innocent blood" can be applied to any actions where innocent people are hurt or destroyed. God hates the violation of the weak by the strong. People of power are not to take advantage of others for their own advancement or to satisfy their own ambition or lusts. Any time the weak and vulnerable are violated, it is cause for God's wrath to come upon the guilty party. Do not become a close associate with a man who is intoxicated with power and wields it either ruthlessly or subtly against those who are vulnerable.

Some people also have ambitious hearts that are politically motivated. When you get close to them, you see that they will do almost anything to get their own way. Such a man "devises wicked schemes" to accomplish what he wants. James warned about people like this: "If you harbor bitter envy and selfish ambition in your hearts, do not boast about it or deny the truth. Such 'wisdom' does not come down from heaven but is earthly, unspiritual, of the devil. For where you have envy and selfish ambition, there you find disorder and every evil practice" (Jas 3:14-16). Wickedness of heart leads to "feet that are quick to rush into evil" (Prov 6:18).

Later in the list is the "false witness." This man will often put a slant on things that damages the reputation of another. Many unstable people in the church are willing to slander another or at least color the truth to give others a negative impression of some person. The title of false witness also fits someone who is quick to pass on second- and third-hand information that may or may not be true. If a person is given to gossip and slander, and you befriend that person, you'll wind up the target sooner or later. Also, accountability is impossible in a relationship where those involved cannot trust in absolute confidentiality.

Why does God hate these things? Because these behaviors stir up dissension and kill relationships in the body of Christ. For example, I have seen good men and women destroyed by the false witness of someone who had a private agenda or an unresolved hurt. Be alert to signs of such behavior. After doing whatever you can to correct the other man's sinful pattern, maintain a wise distance—close enough to help, far enough away so you won't get sucked in.

Men who are evil schemers, liars, gossips and slanderers, bearers of false witness, ambitious power brokers—they are viruses circulating in the body. Minister to them. Love them. Help them see the error in their choices. But don't choose a man like this to be a close friend and spiritual development partner.

WALKING WITH THE WISE

If you want to have wisdom, walk with the wise. Men of godly wisdom will predominately display character qualities that are the opposite of the seven traits God hates. These are the kind of people we should want to spend time with, because they pick us up and build us up, teach us and train us, mentor us, disciple us, hold us accountable, encourage and strengthen us, pray for us, stand by us, walk with us through thick and thin. Their godly character traits, attitudes and actions rub off on us. We all need friends like these.

Instead of arrogance and a haughty attitude, the people we want to be close to will show true humility, a teachable spirit. This kind of person delights in serving and encouraging others. A humble man will show the qualities of Christ in everyday life. These character traits of humility are what James described as having wisdom from above. "The wisdom that comes from heaven is first of all pure; then peace-loving, considerate, submissive, full of mercy and good fruit, impartial and sincere. Peacemakers who sow in peace raise a harvest of righteousness" (Jas 3:17-18).

We should look for friends and accountability partners who will encourage us to be truthful in speech so our lives will demonstrate consistency between what we say and how we behave. We should look for friends who are willing to risk wounding us, if need be, when they see us taking the first steps toward a slide into ruin. "Wounds from a friend can be trusted" (Prov 27:6).

Instead of entering into committed relationships

with men who can be cruel or insensitive, we should look for those who have a compassionate heart. They can grow our compassion for the things that break the heart of God. We should look for those who are advocates of the hurting or powerless, who are willing to sacrifice themselves for the good of the kingdom. These are not men who wield worldly power to get their own way. Rather, they are men who stand in the power of Christ to achieve the best for others, especially for those who have no voice. These are the people we need to cultivate as mentor-friends.

The King James translation of the Bible describes some men as having no guile (see John 1:47). The word *guile* comes from a Greek term that means "a decoy." A man with no guile is not a decoy, not a man living a pretend life—just looking like the authentic article on the outside. A man who has no guile has made genuine progress with God in the power of the Spirit against his selfish motivations. He is humble and grateful to God. He is not a control freak, plotting things behind the scenes. A man with no guile finds it easy to work in submission to authority. We should look for men like this.

We also want to surround ourselves with men who care about morality. If we find a person who is so pure-hearted that just being around him sensitizes our conscience, we should try to get more time with that person. As we cultivate relationships with people of integrity, their integrity will rub off on us.

Instead of loose-tongued people who spread any

gossip anywhere, we want close friends who will never break confidentiality. We want people around us to whom we can bare our soul, knowing that what we say will be kept in confidence. Without this confidence, our growth will stagnate. We will never reach deep levels of self-awareness and core character development unless we share our real lives with friends like these.

Some people seem to naturally create strife. They complain all the time about what others are doing or not doing. They blame others for their own problems. They strike matches to any kindling that exists anywhere and leave a trail of relational fires behind them. Instead of these people, we should seek friends who are reconcilers, forgivers, lovers. We should seek graceful people, peacemakers.

Even good friends will have disagreements. But disagreements are healthy in good relationships, offering opportunities for growth. No disagreement can create dissension in the body unless one of the parties is self-centered, arrogant or stubborn. If both parties are walking in the Spirit of the Lord, they will work out even intense disagreements in an atmosphere of openness and love. That's why we should surround ourselves with people who show a willingness to submit to the Holy Spirit.

Our spiritual development partners should be a few close friends who have humble souls, honest words and lives, serving hands, pure hearts, listening ears, reconciling spirits. Paying attention to these character qualities will help us examine the relationships in our lives. We can use the above-mentioned negative and positive qualities as a guide for seeking God's wisdom in identifying someone who has the potential to develop a mature friendship with us.

We are not looking for a perfect person. No man will fit that bill. And if we or the other man were perfect, there would be no need for an accountable friendship! But when we see good character qualities exhibited with some level of consistency and balance in another's life, the potential is there for a relationship that will work. Most important, though, is the sense of guidance we get after praying for discernment about whether to initiate a more intentional friendship and go deeper in the Lord.

THE BEST ADVICE ON HOW TO FIND A GOOD FRIEND

How do you find a quality person to have as a friend? First of all, you have to be the kind of man whom others would want to add to *their* spiritual development team. Then finding good friends will be easier than you think. Ask yourself this question: *Would another man find in me many of these important qualities necessary for a good friendship?*

When another man shares something private with you and you never spread it around, you begin to be known in your circle of acquaintances as a person who can be trusted. Others will seek you out as a person with whom they can share the deeper life.

If you keep your promises, others who care about honesty in relationships will find you. If you're a good listener with a nonjudgmental spirit, men will seek you out for help and guidance. If you are a man who doesn't take himself too seriously, you will attract men who are serious about their faith but are also able to enjoy their relationships with others. If you are a man who is quick to take the concerns of others to the Father in prayer, you will be sought out by other men who are devoted to prayer. In short, if you are a good candidate yourself for an honest, open relationship as a Christian friend, then you will be sought after by other men eager to be in relationship with you.

FOR REFLECTION OR DISCUSSION

1. One statement in this chapter claims that the most significant things we've learned and retained in life have most likely come through a trusted relationship. How true is this for your life?

2. Think of times in your life when being with the wrong person has hurt you. Also, think of times when being in the right company benefited you. Jot down your recollections or share them with your study partner.

3. The author warns against associating with people who have certain character flaws. Yet we are all sinners, aren't we? How do you understand the author's point?

4. What changes would you need to make in your own life to become the kind of man others would seek out for a friend?

4   ARE YOU READY FOR ACCOUNTABILITY?

THE NEXT WEEK, BILL AND LARRY DECIDED ON the doughnut shop near Larry's office. As they sat at a table against the wall, each man caught the other up on how his week had been going. Then Bill took the conversation in a different direction. "Larry, I've been doing some thinking."

"Uh-oh," Larry said with a smile, "that sounds dangerous."

"No, nothing earth shattering," Bill went on. "I just thought it might be timely for us to talk about some of the . . . what am I trying to say, maybe ground rules? The things we need to pay attention to that will help make this accountability relationship really work."

"That's a good idea," Larry said. "I know what you mean. How to keep our trust and comfort levels growing."

"Right. You've got it."

"We should probably take some notes here." Larry pulled out a pen and tore a blank sheet from his Day-Timer, then clicked his pen in readiness. "Where do we start?"

"Well, a few years ago, I told a friend about a family matter that needed to stay private between us, for my family's sake. And a couple of weeks later someone else at church

came up to me to ask how we were all doing with it."

"Ouch."

"Yeah, and more than one person mentioned it! I think this guy told his whole small group about it, as a 'prayer concern.' Yikes! It was all over the church. I talked with him about how he had hurt me in spreading it around. He apologized, but I still have a hard time opening up about stuff now."

"That's awful," Larry empathized. "I sure don't ever want to do anything like that to you. Nothing you say here leaves here, not even if it seems trivial or casual. Not unless you give me the go-ahead to talk about it openly."

"Thanks. I appreciate it."

"And it goes both ways, right?" Larry asked. "I mean, you don't tell anyone about the stuff I tell you?"

"Nope. Not even to Diane. What's said here stays here. Otherwise we won't feel we can really open up to each other."

Larry nodded and scribbled some more notes on his paper.

Then Bill said, "You know, we've talked about this already, but I really appreciate the honesty in sharing. That's another ingredient. We should always try to give the most honest answers we can. It's too easy to talk about surface things without getting to the real issues."

"Yeah, that's definitely true," Larry agreed. "I'll try to be as honest as I can be when I'm answering questions you ask me, even in tough areas. That's hard for me, so you'll have to be patient. I've been a Lone Ranger for a long time. I haven't done a lot of opening up, even though I know it's what I need most.

"Oh, I have to tell you, I really appreciate that you'll just pick up the phone occasionally and call me, just to check in. That is really so meaningful to me. I've never had that."

"That's part of the deal," Bill said. *"Being available to each other, making our friendship a high priority timewise— that's what it's all about."*

"More ingredients," Larry nodded, smiling. *"You know, these things I'm writing down remind me of taking my wedding vows."*

"I know," Bill laughed. *"But these are covenants we're making. It's serious, isn't it? The quality of our relationship depends on these things."*

"We couldn't do this—I mean the honesty and vulnerability and even having the courage to challenge each other—we couldn't do this if we didn't have God in our corner. 'I will never leave you nor forsake you!' That's his covenant with us," Larry said.

"And we're actually saying that to each other here, too, aren't we, Larry?"

"Wow! That's true. And that's heavy, huh?"

Bill reached over and took Larry's note sheet. He signed his name at the bottom. Then he said, *"There. I make this promise, to do the best I can to live up to these things."*

"And I make the same promise," Larry said, signing his own name. *"But I also promise,"* Larry went on, *"to forgive you when you fall short and to always let you begin again."*

"You have my word on that too," Bill finished up.

Larry's pen stuck to his doughnut-sticky fingers when he

tried to set it down. He had to shake it off onto the table. Both men laughed and then stood, gave each other a hug, said good-bye and headed off to work.

I begin this chapter with a sense of urgency about the importance of the material included here. This chapter talks about the character qualities and commitments we bring to the accountability relationship. These are the essential ingredients that will determine whether accountability works or fails. Without bringing honesty, vulnerability and teachability to the table, for instance, accountability cannot possibly achieve the spiritual growth and health we seek.

I have known men who, I had no doubt, believed wholeheartedly in accountability and participated regularly in accountable relationships, yet still fell into sin in some significant area of their Christian lives. I have wondered, *how can this possibly happen?*

One pastor I knew met weekly with an elder from his church who asked him all the right questions about the integrity of his relationships. This pastor was involved in a men's small group where they often discussed topics like sexual purity. He was in a confidential, personal prayer group designed to give him a safe place where he could be open and receive the support he needed in his ministry or personal life. But while he was engaged in this network of accountable relationships, he was at the same time participating in hidden sin that would eventually destroy his ministry.

The reason I carry today a deeper sense of urgency regarding the seriousness with which we approach our accountable relationships is that I have recently experienced a similar contradiction in my own life. I write the books on accountability and do the seminars and pastors' conferences on resisting temptation. I have for years involved myself in accountable friendships and men's small groups for study and prayer to help me stay fresh and alive and safe in the Lord.

But recently I found myself entangled in a friendship relationship that blew up and created pain for a number of people. There was no moral failure here. But the situation had subtle elements to it that carried the potential for misunderstanding and emotional pain. I should have seen it coming but didn't. If I had been more alert and paid more attention to some of the early warning signs—especially if I had opened up the questionable areas earlier to my accountability partner—the pain this situation created for myself, Judie, my family and others would most certainly have been avoided.

Rationalization and denial are powerful forces in all of our lives. The smarter we are, the easier it seems to be for us to talk ourselves into something. We are all good at creating convincing arguments that can work to ease our conscience about some questionable practice that's giving us something we want or feel we need. I won't be as quick in the future to judge others who are caught in this contradiction. But I will be wiser myself and even more deeply committed to the principles in this chapter that are the foundation for effective and practical accountability. The apostle Paul's warning is now burned into my awareness: "So, if you think you are standing firm, be careful that you don't fall!" (1 Cor 10:12).

I have already mentioned that honesty, vulnerability and teachability are essential to effective accountability. But there are other commitments you also need to bring to an accountability relationship if it is going to be effective. You have to make yourself available to your accountability partner. You have to maintain strict confidentiality about things shared between you. You also have to be dependable and loyal, a man who will stand by his friends, not desert them when the going gets rough.

Let's look at some of the qualities now in greater detail.

VULNERABILITY

Vulnerability is a quality of conscience. It is reflected in the man who is sensitive, able to be wounded by personal sin, willing to be shown where he is wrong. It is the quality identified in 1 Timothy 1:5 as having "a pure heart and a good conscience and a sincere faith." A sign that a man is maturing in this quality of conscience is that he will be quick to admit sin and error even before he is confronted with his wrongdoing.

Vulnerability describes a willingness to open one's life up to another. This is an area of struggle for most men. If we are at all insecure about ourselves, we will be tempted to project an image that isn't accurate or honest. We will be tempted to cover up the truth or color our life situation to make ourselves look better. We might admit a certain area as a trouble spot in our lives, but then we pretend to make progress in this area when we're really up against a wall.

The cure to the cover-up, of course, is knowing that we are already accepted and approved by God. Once I have internalized the fact that I am unconditionally loved by the only One who really matters, I am set free from having to convince myself or others that I am worth something. I am freed forever from having to cover up my inadequacies.

In Christ I do not have to perform perfectly to be loved. Forgiveness is active in my life, therefore I can admit openly that I often fail. This vulnerability is the foundation on which accountability rests. We are all in the same place in Christ. We are all forgiven sinners in need of a lot of grace and help. What would be the point of saying we are interested in growing in Christ and then covering up areas where the growth most needs to take place? A mature man recognizes his need to grow and learn. A free man exhibits vulnerability by admitting his needs and accepting the help, advice and support of others.

TEACHABILITY

If you are teachable, you are open to counsel from others and are quick to hear and respond to reproof. Learning how to give and receive loving counsel is essential for a man who wants to become mature in Christ and help others to grow. Remember, "as iron sharpens iron, so one man sharpens another" and "wounds from a friend can be trusted" (Prov 27:17, 6). Of course, we are talking here about constructive criticism. This is correction, advice and counsel coming to you from men who have already demonstrated their love for you, men you know you can trust.

The Bible assumes that you and I will be involved in this process of mutual training and reproof. "All Scripture is God-breathed and is useful for teaching, rebuking, correcting and training in righteousness, so that the man of God may be thoroughly equipped for every good work" (2 Tim 3:16-17). If we really want to be thoroughly equipped for the work of God, we will desire the training in righteousness that comes to us through the loving correction of others.

We are good at deceiving ourselves (Jer 17:9). Therefore, we need the objective critique of others to keep us on track. I remember how, when I was fresh out of college and beginning my teaching career, I arrogantly thought I was God's gift to the teaching profession. I'm sure I did have some gifts, but I also had many blind spots. The principal called me in after I had been teaching in that junior high school for about three months. I still remember distinctly his words, which gave me a dose of reality. He said, "You have the potential to be one of the best teachers in our program. But if you don't learn how to discipline your students, I will not renew your contract next year."

That got my attention. But to his credit, he didn't just drop the bomb and throw me out of his office. He offered his help, his time and his expertise so that I could learn some important things. He asked if he could visit my classroom a couple of times a week, just to observe how I handled things. I welcomed his help. Then we would meet after school on those days and he would share from his experience things I might have done differently.

Within a few weeks, I had learned so many helpful strategies from him that teaching became a joy. My classrooms were finally under such good control that I could effectively deploy my gifts. I was enjoying real success in teaching rather than just imaginary success.

That principal was a good friend, willing to risk giving me a rebuke for the sake of my personal growth and professional future. And he was willing to work with me through the changes. I learned more from him than just how to discipline junior high kids; he is a model for me of what a good accountability partner will do.

Sometimes, too, we just need a good kick in the pants. We know what's right to do, but we're being lazy or procrastinating. When that's the case, it's time for a bit of correction from a friend. I remember another occasion when I had been working on a book project for over three years. I wanted to be finished. I was tired. My editor's opinion was that I still had work to do. I objected, but he said, "It's not good enough." I'll never forget his letter to me at that time and the little phrase he used: "Faithful are the wounds of a good editor." He knew how to get the best out of me when I was tempted to settle for less.

A good friend who wants to hold you accountable has your best interests in mind. A man who enters into this sort of relationship with you believes in you, trusts you, knows your heart for God. But he also will have an eye for your limitations. He will be objective about areas where you need to grow. After all, what do you really want? It is to continue to make progress toward maturity in Christ, isn't it? We don't get anywhere if we surround ourselves with people who just tell us what we want to hear.

In both cases I mentioned above (disciplining students and revising a book), I needed to be willing to listen to the correction and respond positively to the challenge to give more. Our attitude should always be a desire to stay focused on our call in Christ and work to improve our character, commitment or effectiveness. That's what it means to have a teachable spirit. The only really harmful mistake we will ever make is refusing to admit and learn from our mistakes. Constructive criticism is such a good thing for us that we should be eager for it, seek it and remain open to understanding more every day about how we can be better equipped to serve God.

HONESTY

The accountable man is committed to telling the truth regardless of how much it hurts. It takes tremendous courage to admit our struggles to others, especially when they are difficult or humiliating. The honest man, however, hates all that is phony or false. He develops a strong distaste for image creating or hypocrisy in lifestyle.

Our willingness to be honest in what we report is at the heart of our accountability relationship. The apostle James wrote, "Confess your sins to each other and pray for each other so that you may be healed" (Jas 5:16). Your accountability partner may ask you a question that really touches a nerve. You may for the moment lack the courage to answer with clarity and honesty. It is all right to promise an answer at the next meeting and to let God strengthen you in prayer so that you can bring this area fully into the light. But don't postpone an honest answer to play the rationalization game. It won't help you, your relationship with your friend or your relationship with God. God hates liars.

All good accountability relationships are built on trust. Your accountability partner has to be able to trust that when he asks you a question, you will answer it truthfully to the best of your ability. You need to be able to trust him in the same way. Nothing is gained by deceit. Everything is gained by honesty and openness.

King David was hiding his sin of power abuse and adultery with Bathsheba, and he was covering up his murder of her husband, Uriah. But when he was confronted by the prophet Nathan, he no longer tried to hide his guilt but instead simply said, "I have sinned against the LORD" (2 Sam 12:13). Nathan assured him then that he was forgiven by God. His confession to Nathan and to God brought joy back into his life.

David wrote of this incident in Psalm 32. He reported, "When I kept silent, my bones wasted away through my groaning all day long" (v. 3). In other words, when he tried to hide his sin, his pain was multiplied. But Nathan came along. "Then I acknowledged my sin to you and did not cover up my iniquity . . . and you forgave the guilt of my sin" (v. 5). David confessed his sin and brought it to light, taking responsibility for his wrongdoing. When he did, God "covered" his sin (v. 1).

A beautiful truth is captured in these verses. If we're trying to hide our faults, problems and sins, they will eventually catch up to us—and often the pain multiplies in time. But if we uncover our sins, God will cover them with his forgiveness.

It pays to be an honest man, to confess our sins to God and others. The apostle Paul said that by "speaking the truth in love, we will in all things grow up into him who is the Head, that is, Christ" (Eph 4:15).

ACCESSIBILITY

When you enter into an accountable relationship, you make a commitment to be there for your partner. You will need to schedule regular times to meet, but accountable friends also commit themselves to responding quickly during times of special need. There is no

way you can have a deep and meaningful relationship
with a friend if you're not willing to give the necessary
time to develop that relationship.

Accessibility also means that you're willing to work
through problems the other man may be having. My
model for this was the principal I mentioned earlier. He
saw an area in my life that needed work. He was willing to speak with me about it directly. But he also
walked with me all the way through the learning period until I was able to stand strong again on my own
two feet.

We need to make ourselves available in practical
ways too, to be a part of the solution to any problem
that might occur in our partner's life. I have always
loved the statement Jonathan made to David in 1 Sam-
uel 20:4: "Whatever you want me to do, I'll do for you."
He was saying, "I'm committed to this relationship,
even if it is going to cost me. Anything I have—time, energy, insight, possessions—is yours if you need it, to the
limit of my resources." We offer ourselves to our partner by being a good listener, by providing prayer support and by being willing to advise and confront.
Relationships that are worth something come at a price.

My wife, Judie, and I lost our first baby in the fifth
month of the pregnancy. When Judie went in for the
surgery and I was crying in agony over the fact that a
tumor had killed our child, Tom was there for me. He
didn't offer advice; he was just there to hear me out, to
sit with me, to put his arm around me. Tom was there
again two years later when our son, Gabe, was born.

He got out of bed when I called him at 2:30 a.m. to join me at a small restaurant in Rochester, Minnesota. We sat together there in the early morning, eating potato pancakes as I told him everything I could think of about the birth. A quality accountability friendship offers this mutual, caring availability to one another.

TRUSTWORTHINESS

The rule is, nothing shared inside the relationship gets shared outside the relationship unless permission has been given. Even small things that seem of no consequence must be held in confidence. That's because real, open and honest life sharing cannot take place unless you can be trusted to keep this personal information private. If you are not trustworthy in this regard, your partner will not be able to open his life to you. And unless you can trust your partner, you will be guarded in what you are willing to reveal. Absolute confidentiality is essential if accountability is going to work.

Men and women often express surprise when they have mentioned something to me—even if it was just in casual conversation—and later they find out Judie knows nothing about it. It isn't that Judie and I don't get enough time to talk. I just learned a long time ago not to share any information of a personal nature that's been given to me. As a result, people know they can come to me with confidential information and that even my closest friend in all the world—my wife—will not be told.

It is easy to let information we're holding slip into

conversations we have with others. The discipline of maintaining control over our tongues in this area may be the most important habit we develop to ensure success in an accountable relationship. I find that I am constantly bridling my tongue when some piece of information about someone pops into my mind. I just stop for a second and ask myself, *Is it necessary for me to add this to the conversation?* Usually I just keep my mouth shut. That sort of hesitation before speaking can keep us out of a lot of trouble. And when our accountability friend comes to know that we have discipline in this area, there will be no impediment to the deeper sharing of our lives together.

EMPATHY

The best accountability partners are men who have experienced real life and are not shocked by the deeper struggles their partners choose to reveal. A person who fears real life cannot foster in others an open relationship with God.

You will be a better accountability friend to another if you understand what it is like to be weakened and feel defeated. Personal experiences of pain and struggle will deepen your compassion for a struggling friend. And because you have experienced real-life difficulties and pain, you understand how God works to bring his comfort and strength in times of deep distress. The apostle Paul said it this way: "Praise be to the God and Father of our Lord Jesus Christ, the Father of compassion and the God of all comfort, who comforts us in all our troubles, so that we can comfort those in any trouble with the comfort we ourselves have received from God" (2 Cor 1:3-4).

An effective accountability partner is able to maintain a helpful level of optimism even though he has tasted the pain of sin and failure. Each of us has failed and still does fail, but we have also experienced salvation, renewal and freedom. While we don't want to be blind to sinful tendencies in ourselves or in our partners, we must have a firm grasp on the truth that "the one who is in you [the Holy Spirit] is greater than the one who is in the world [the devil]" (1 John 4:4). It pays to remember that no matter how dark the darkness gets, it cannot overcome the light. We have this hope to offer a struggling friend.

However formidable the power of sin may seem, the resurrection power available to us is more formidable still. The apostle Paul prayed in Ephesians that our eyes would be opened and that we would realize that we have an "incomparably great power" at work within us. It is the same power that God "exerted in Christ when he raised him from the dead" (Eph 1:18-21). We have resurrection power available to us to live the Christian life. This is the imperishable hope that brothers have to share with each other as they walk the journey toward maturity in Christ.

The gift of confidence in Christ we hold out to each other along the way is what brings the light of promise into our relationship so that, shoulder to shoulder, we will have the courage to take the next bold, hopeful step.

FOR REFLECTION OR DISCUSSION

1. As you consider the character qualities important to the success of an accountable friendship, which ones seem the hardest for you to live out? How might you be able to change past patterns to strengthen these areas?

2. Which of the qualities do you believe you possess in good measure? How do you know this?

3. How does receiving the unconditional acceptance of God free you to be more open and vulnerable about your struggles?

4. Do you believe you are the kind of man who can listen to an honest confession of a spiritually wounded friend and respond with love, compassion and hope? In an attitude of prayer, let the Lord search your heart in this.

5

THE PRIMARY SKILL
                              Listening Well

*TWO WEEKS LATER LARRY AND BILL were back at the pancake
house. Larry stirred his coffee listlessly and kept staring out
the window. He hadn't eaten a bite but just kept moving his
cold eggs around on his plate. Finally he spoke.* "Bill, I've
been trying to get my courage up for several weeks now to
talk to you about something where I really need help."

Bill nodded. "Okay."

"And it involves someone else. So you know how important privacy is here."

"I think you know I'm committed to that."

*Larry looked down, then to the side, and finally took a
deep breath and jumped into it.* "I'm friends with someone at
church," *he started.* "A woman. You probably know her.
Connie. Do you know her? And her husband, Ed?"

"I know who they are, but I don't know them well. They
seem like a really nice couple."

"They are. I totally agree." *Larry stopped.* "Well, our
families spend a lot of time together because we're neighbors,
friends. We do things together."

Larry paused. Bill waited until he could make eye contact.

"Larry, what are we talking about here?" he asked. "What's going on?"

Larry took a deep breath and said, "It's not like we're having an affair or anything. But there's something between Connie and me. It's an attraction thing that has a lot of power in it. I know it's mutual, but we have never spoken about it. I don't do anything to advance the thing. Neither does Connie, thank God. It has just grown because of the time our families spend together."

"How do you know that she feels the same way?"

"Well, it's mainly that she does things around me that women do when they're near a man they have feelings for. It's like a seductive kind of closeness you can feel even sitting across a room full of people. I can tell we both want to be there even if we're not talking. It's the eye contact." He paused and looked uncomfortable.

Bill waited.

"And, you know, she'll touch me on occasion. We hug. All of us do. We've been friends for years. But Connie touches me like a woman touches a man she loves. Like just walking by, the light touch on the arm and the hesitation."

"Larry, it sounds like you're feeling kind of out of control," Bill said, "like you're lost in this and don't know how to get a handle on it."

"I need to say this first, about Karen. I am incredibly in love with my wife. She makes my heart pump. She's a beautiful woman in every way. I love her touch, the smell of her hair, the way she turns to me when I'm near her. That's what's so weird *about this, that this other attraction can be going on, but I'm still so totally attracted to and in love with my wife."*

"I believe you, Larry. I'm glad to hear about your commitment to Karen. But you also have this powerful sexual tension going on with Connie."

"It's been scary to me. What's different about her is that she communicates this interest in me so subtly. And on the other hand, she maintains this strict distance. And that's what feels so seductive to me."

"It sounds like it can get overpowering at times, Larry."

"I do feel overpowered, out of control. That's why I really needed to talk about this."

Both men paused thoughtfully. Then Bill reflected, "It seems like you are not in control of the relationship and that Connie is not a person who can be controlled. Like she is in the seat of power in a way. That's worth thinking about. What is your fantasy life like? What happens with you and Connie in your head?"

"What's going on in my head is pretty innocent. I find myself daydreaming about her, but we're just having a conversation together, in some nice spot, walking along a beach or sitting inside by a fire on a snowy day, enjoying each other's company."

"Does it go further than that?"

"No. Part of what keeps this going is that I really don't have sexual fantasies about Connie. I think about her being attractive, that kind of stuff. But I don't really dwell on anything sexual there. If my thoughts toward her were typical

guy thoughts, I don't think I could tolerate it. But somehow thinking about her the way I do seems okay. But I probably think about her too much. I know it's not good for me to be thinking about her at all. And my guess is that she is thinking too much about me too."

"How so?"

"We were chatting for a minute by the mailbox the other day, and she mentioned something I had said to her probably a year and a half ago. I mean, she is remembering and holding these little conversations in her head."

"And you feel flattered by that."

Larry thought for a moment. "Hmm. Yeah, I guess you're right. Wow! That's part of this I wasn't seeing. But it hits home."

"Well, when an attractive woman pays special attention to us in that way, it can light up the male ego. And isn't she about ten years younger than you?"

"Yeah, she is. This might be more about me than I want to admit." Larry seemed to be breathing a little easier just talking about it.

Then Bill suggested, "Next time, maybe we could talk about what your behavior toward Connie would look like if you really loved her as a sister in Christ rather than as a romantic fantasy.

"I know this is really scary," Bill continued, looking Larry in the eye, "but you may need to think about sharing some of this with Karen. I'm sure you're worried about Karen and Connie and their friendship, but our wives can be sur-

prisingly understanding about this kind of stuff. Sharing it with Karen could stop the thing cold."

"Wow! That's something I'll pray about, all right."

"Meanwhile, I'll keep my eye on you, okay? If you have inappropriate thoughts about Connie this week, remember that I'm going to ask you about it next week. That will probably help to cool the flame."

"That's the help I'm looking for."

As Bill picked up the check, he said, "Larry, I need to say how much I admire your courage and honesty. And thank you for trusting me with this. I have a feeling that God is going to get some good work done here because you had the courage to open up."

"Thanks for listening, Bill."

At this point you might be wondering whether you are up to the task of being in an accountable relationship with another Christian man. The character qualities listed in the last chapter can seem overwhelming. If you were to give yourself a score from 1 to 10 (10 being high on each of those qualities), you might honestly mark yourself somewhere in the middle on most of them. And so you are tempted to wonder whether you dare take this step toward deeper commitment to God and to a friend or small group of men. You are wondering whether you are as open and honest a man as this relationship may call you to be.

Before you decide you're not ready for this, I would like to encourage you. If you have anxiety or feelings of inadequacy, I think I can help you by describing better your role in this spiritual friendship to which God may be calling you.

The most important thing to keep in mind is that you are not the one who is ultimately responsible for the life change that will occur as you and your friend journey together. You are not your friend's savior; God shoulders that responsibility. Remember, "he who began a good work in you will carry it on to completion until the day of Christ Jesus" (Phil 1:6). God brought life to you and your friend, and God is at work in both of you to bring about growth and change. He will get his work done. That is a promise you can trust.

Let God be God in your friendship, and you will immediately experience freedom from performance anxiety and from the burden of worrying that you are going to do some irreversible harm to the relationship. Keep these things in mind:

- Who will bring wisdom from above to you and your friend? The Lord (Jas 1:5).

- Who will lavish love and life-changing forgiveness

on you and your friend when you're struggling? The Lord (1 Jn 1:8-9).

- Who can you count on to shine a bright light on the next step you need to take as you journey with God? The Lord (Ps 48:14).

- If all this is true, then who should both of you be listening for before you speak to each other in this accountable friendship? The Lord.

LISTENING IS THE HEART OF THE MATTER

If we can keep reminding ourselves that the real work in our relationship is God's, then we can see our relationship as being one of companions in search of God's voice for each other's lives. The value of having a companion is that your friend will see things you may miss. Likewise, you will often see things he may miss.

The primary skill that men in accountable relationships need to learn is the skill of listening well. We do not need to be experts in anything except the down-to-earth humility that acknowledges God's power and presence as central to all of life. A simple willingness on the part of the men involved to search the Scriptures and to be in prayer for each other opens the door for God to speak his life-changing word.

It is often true, though, that the simplest thing turns out to be harder than it seems. Learning to listen well to God and to our friends takes a kind of discipline that is hard for us as men. We have been conditioned to think in terms of suggesting quick solutions to problems. For many of us, our livelihood depends on being analytical, objective, decisive. We are often affirmed when we demonstrate these qualities.

But when it is God's solution we seek with our friend, we need to take the time to pray and give space for the Holy Spirit to lead. James warned that we need to be "quick to listen, slow to speak" (Jas 1:19). The apostle expanded on his point by adding, "If anyone considers himself religious and yet does not keep a tight rein on his tongue, he deceives himself" (v. 26). In our eagerness to help we will always have to fight the temptation to judge a situation too quickly, to jump ahead of God and try to bring a quick fix out of our limited experience, or to slap on an ill-fitting Scripture.

This kind of immaturity risks damaging our relationship with our friend who is hurt because we have not listened well. Our superficial response doesn't help; it just adds to his pain. We have to keep a tight rein not only on our tongues but also on our egos. I often say that E.G.O. stands for Edging God Out. That's what we do when we don't listen long and prayerfully enough before taking action regarding a situation in our friend's life.

I like a parable attributed to Paphnutius, one of the wise old desert fathers. He said one day he saw a man on the bank of a river sunk to his knees in mud. Some friends came to help him out, but they wound up pushing him farther in—up to his neck! It reminds me of the bad advice Job got from superficial friends who thought they knew exactly what they were doing.

We need to remember that the only help that is real help originates in God. God has to be the source of what we do or say to another or else we will do nothing more than mess up our friend's life. That is why it is so crucial to learn and practice the skill of prayerful listening when we meet together in an accountable relationship.

THE PRACTICE OF GODLY LISTENING

The first thing to do when you are ready to open up life issues with your friend or in your small group of men is to create a space for God. Often you have been enjoying fellowship, sharing and getting caught up on things together. But then as you enter into a time to listen together for God's word to you, stop and be silent together. Let the silence be a relaxed silence. (You get more comfortable with silence the more you practice it.) The silence can be broken then by one or the other praying out loud as the Lord leads, followed by the beginning of your conversation. Or one or the other of you can just start talking as something seems to surface.

If your friend begins, be attentive to what he is saying verbally as well as through his body language. Also, pay attention to what is going on in yourself as he is telling you of his experience. Look for God to give you clues about what might be at the heart of the matter.

When your friend is speaking, make him your focus, even though this may mean giving up your desire to be the center of attention. But it is important that you hear— really hear—your friend. There may be no other place in the world where he is given this kind of undivided attention. When you listen like this to another, you say through your action that there is nothing more important in the world to you at that moment. You are there for him, and you are committed to helping him hear the Lord for whatever circumstance he has chosen to talk about.

Listen for words that get repeated. They may be clues to the heart of the matter for your friend. Over time, you may hear certain stories come up again and again. These repetitions may be prompted by the Holy Spirit. There is something in these particular stories that offers a clue to how the Lord wants to bring freedom to your friend in some area of confusion, weakness or struggle.

You may experience a particular emotion as your friend is sharing his heart. God may be leading you to say something as simple as "When I heard you tell that story about you and your brother, I felt loneliness." It is always amazing to me how these small things often turn out to be a key from God to unlock what has lain behind a sealed door in the other man's life. And the sharing then goes deeper into what really needs to be talked about and released.

I live in the gold country of the California Sierras. Some years ago I got into recreational mining and gold panning. One of my gold buddies is a former Navy SEAL who has tremendous observational skills and a kind of sixth sense about where the gold lies. It's a great experience for me to work a stream with Bill, watching him gather the clues that tell him where digging will be most productive.

Accountability friends are like two miners looking for gold buried somewhere beneath the surface in each other's lives. As we go along together, we develop greater skills of observation and spiritual intuition. Our "sixth sense" about things is the leading of the Holy Spirit. He is active in the relationship, giving clues to each man as to where it might be most productive to dig. The Lord also helps us to know when some "lead" is really nothing more than a dead end—when it isn't going to "pan out."

Spiritual discernment grows in a good relationship the longer two men journey together in the Lord. Discernment is having the spiritual confidence to make a choice to go one way or another with a conversation. The longer you practice listening well to each other and to God in your friendship, the better you will become at noticing where God is moving a discussion. You learn to pursue deeper what feels like life to the both of you. That's the vein of emotional gold you follow together.

Searching for gold is delicate work requiring the skills of observation and intuition, and so is learning to listen well to each other and to God in a mutual relationship of accountability.

TYPICAL MALE BARRIERS TO LISTENING WELL

The admonition from James to be "quick to listen" and "slow to speak" seems to me to be especially appropriate for men. Most of us men need to hold back on our temptation to suggest a quick solution before we really understand the problem. God will lead us to the heart of the matter, but we have to be patient. It seems to be a part of our male ego to want to tell somebody else what to do.

God is amazingly creative in the diversity of ways he works in people. The answer that was perfect for you in a particular area of your personal growth may not work at all with your friend. His situation may be just different enough that it has to be treated with an entirely different divine strategy. That's why listening well is so important. We always need to stay disciplined enough that we don't jump to conclusions about something we're hearing.

The goal is not to try to make your partner be more like you but to help your partner become everything he can be in the Lord according to his uniqueness as a man of God. The calling God has placed on you for your friend's life requires that your listening and discernment be guided by the Holy Spirit.

Your mature patience and demonstrated acceptance of God's diverse ways of working allows your partner to be himself. The result is that his faith in you as a friend, and his observation that you're allowing God to take the initiative, build trust and a willingness to open up to you even more.

Silence your story. The first thing you'll need to work on is silencing the tendency to insert your own story. On a superficial hearing of your friend's situation, something in it may seem similar enough to something you experienced that you have the urge to jump in with your story. When that urge comes, do a spiritual counting to ten. Ask God whether you should speak your experience into the dialogue or bite your tongue for a bit.

Often, if you have the patience to wait it out, you'll be thankful you did. Your friend's story will take an unexpected turn a moment later, and you will realize that what you had thought about saying would have missed the mark. By listening prayerfully, carefully and patiently to your partner, you will let your friend know that you want to *really* hear him and that you're not interested in speaking or taking action until you sense the leading of God. This is how trust grows in a relationship.

Whenever you hear yourself saying, "That reminds me of . . ." or "I had exactly that same . . . ," be careful. You're on the verge of diminishing the uniqueness of your friend's experience and taking the focus off him and putting it on yourself. Learn to silence your own story.

Silence the fixer. We seem to have an innate urge to fix the other person's problem. But the best way for real change to take place in our partner is for *him* to discover what his next step needs to be. If we truly believe that God is at work in our partner's life, we should be looking for ways to encourage his search for God's solution, rather than risk jumping in ahead of God with some quick fix of our own. We have to learn better how to live for a while with the uncomfortable feeling that is generated in us by our sharing our partner's pain. What does God want here? That's the question.

The fixer in us gets in the way of good listening. We want so much to help. We root around in our minds for advice we could give. But as soon as we become involved in this fix-it activity, we've stopped listening. We have concluded that we already understand the problem, and now we're focused inward, on our wanting to help.

The most important thing you can do for a friend is to let him learn better how to hear God in his circumstance. Sometimes such simple questions as "Have you asked God how he feels about this?" or "What would you like God to do for you in this circumstance?" can help your friend stay focused on his relationship with the Lord, rather than becoming dependent on you for solving his problems.

Silence the preacher. Just as we are prone to throw in an ill-fitting story from our own experience, so we are also tempted to force into the conversation an ill-fitting Scripture or teaching we have heard or used before. We who like to talk, teach and preach are especially likely to dominate conversations in this way. Feeling like we have the answer for others can be gratifying to our ego. But the warnings from James apply here too:

> If anyone considers himself religious and yet does not keep a tight reign on his tongue, he deceives himself and his religion is worthless. (Jas 1:26)

> Not many of you should presume to be teachers, my brothers, because you know that we who teach will be judged more strictly. We all stumble in many ways. (Jas 3:1-2)

If you know that you tend to talk too much, that you are proud of the Scripture you know or that you tend to think you have the answers for other people, then be cautious in this area. Give your partner permission to interrupt you at any point when your verbal or scriptural stream becomes an overwhelming flood. That's when your partner can say, "You're preaching at me again!"

The mature Christian man trusts that God is at work, so he is able to hold at bay his own experience, his prejudices, his judgment, and his ego's need to speak and be heard. He is able to compassionately enter into the world of his partner and to discern where God is leading his friend—and to join him there.

You and your partner can help each other in these areas by holding one another accountable for practicing good listening skills.

SPECIAL LISTENING: HEARING A FRIEND'S CONFESSION

One unique listening role we play for one another in a mature accountability relationship is the priestly role of hearing each other's confessions of sin. Scripture says, "Confess your sins to each other and pray for each other so that you may be healed" (Jas 5:16).

I learned an important spiritual principle at one time in my life through a painful physical experience. A car ran a stop sign and hit me nearly head-on while I was on my motorcycle. My injuries were extensive. I remember the nurse who was working on my torn-up right leg, trying to clean it with a sponge. The leg was opened up with a number of large lacerations, and sand, dirt and small bits of blacktop were embedded in the wounds. The sponge wasn't getting it all out, so the nurse warned me she would have to use the stiff brush. She said simply, "It has to be clean for it to heal."

Getting clean can be a painful experience. It was for me that day. But I have always remembered the nurse's little phrase and have thought how true it is in the spiritual realm. All healing requires cleansing.

When all else is stripped away, God is what we really want and need. And it is always the case that sin separates us from God. When we confess our sin, we open the door for God's love to rush in. The open wound is cleaned up through forgiveness and treated with the love and grace of God, then continued exposure to light and fresh air through confession brings about further healing and ultimate wholeness.

The cleansing role the nurse played for me physically is the same role we play with a friend spiritually when he is weighed down under a burden of sin. We help in bringing about the cleansing and healing by encouraging our brother to release the burden he is carrying. And that begins by giving a loving invitation to him to speak about what is troubling him.

My experience is that we all want to come clean and receive the healing that comes from God. Confession is painful to do, but there is in it an immediate sense of relief when we give permission for our friend to bring his sin into the light. And with continued prayer support and accountability, our friend will experience complete healing and full restoration.

It is not that we have to speak our sins out loud to another person before forgiveness can take place. The priestly system with a human mediator between sinners and God was done away with when Jesus gave his life once for all on the cross. We have personal, immediate access to the forgiveness of God (1 Jn 1:8-9). But there is something beautiful about how God has designed the body of Christ so that meaningful life sharing takes place in important areas like confession and absolution. The apostle Paul wrote, "Carry each other's burdens, and in this way you will fulfill the law of Christ" (Gal 6:2).

When you hear your brother's confession, you help lift the burden from him. Help your brother name the sin. And then be ready to speak a loving absolution. You may even want to rise at a point like this and lay hands on your brother. In an attitude of prayer, say: "What you have just told me is a confession. The Bible says we are to confess our sins to one another so that we may receive God's forgiveness and healing. I am convinced that you are truly sorry for this. Therefore, in the name of Jesus Christ, your sins are forgiven."

In Matthew 16:19 the Lord talks to Peter about binding and loosing. He says, in effect, that whatever Peter would bind on earth would have been bound in heaven, and whatever Peter would loose on earth would have been loosed in heaven. It is a highly debated passage. I believe that the essence of its meaning is that we have the freedom to offer one another any promises and realities that have already been accomplished for us by the power of heaven. Because forgiveness has been established through the work of the cross of Christ and promised in Scripture to all who sincerely repent of their sin, we can confidently offer God's forgiveness to one another in the name of Christ. And so we act in this priestly way in each other's life, and after offering the above absolution, we can say, "Go in peace, my friend."

In order for you and your accountability partner to be willing to open your lives to each other at this level, you must both be convinced that the other will hear you with compassion and love. You have to be certain that your partner will not be shocked or offended by your admission of sin. And he has to be sure of that in you. To know the truth about a brother and to love him where he needs love the most—that takes great maturity.

We need to remember what the gospel is all about. The good news is that no matter who we are, no matter what we've done, God loves us and offers forgiveness if we are truly sorry for our sin. What we need most at our lowest point is not someone to tell us we have done wrong; it is not judgment by another; it is not even "fixing." What we need most is to know the love and acceptance of Christ. This kind of help does not give us permission to continue in our sin, but it does give us the strength we need to go on in our battle. None of us fights well if we feel that we are already defeated.

Even a casual reading of the Gospels should convince us that Jesus has a special feeling in his heart for the hurting, the lost and the weak. It is the one sheep that strays that receives his attention. He offers love and forgiveness to prostitutes, adulterers, thieves and crooks. And one of his most famous teachings is about a young man who squandered his family inheritance on foolish, riotous living. When the young man woke up to his condition, the father was there waiting, eager to welcome him home again (Luke 15:11-24). There is always hope and a fresh start for the man who knows his sin and is willing to repent of it.

Our priestly help to one another has to come in the style of Jesus. Our words of absolution to one another, offered in the name of Christ, are what the good news is all about. Our love has to be unconditional, our forgiveness a bottomless well of living water, as we stand side by side together, sharing with each other the life and grace of God.

FOR REFLECTION OR DISCUSSION

1. Reread the Scriptures listed in the opening paragraphs of this chapter, then summarize in your own words what you believe are their most helpful ideas.

2. How many reasons can you think of why good listening is a wonderful gift to give a friend?

3. This chapter mentions a number of barriers that get in the way of listening well. Which ones do you struggle with the most? How can you become a better listener?

4. Reflect on your comfort level in hearing another man's confession and offering him the hope of forgiveness that is promised in Christ. Are you willing to be the bearer of this good news to a hurting friend?

6

LOVING CONFRONTATION

FOR A CHANGE OF PACE, Larry met at Bill's house one Saturday morning. Diane and the kids were out of town visiting her mom. Bill demonstrated his expertise at making omelets while Larry carried on the conversation. "Bill, I want to just say again how thankful I've been that we decided to start meeting together when we did."

Bill whisked the eggs and milk together in a large blue bowl.

Larry continued, "These times are always good for me, meaningful and helpful. Driving over this morning, I remembered that we agreed that we were going to reevaluate the relationship on a date that came and went a few months ago. Neither of us has even noticed."

"I know, Larry. It's been really good for me too. I'm learning so much about the value of friendship. I thought I knew it all, but I'm getting things from this relationship that I didn't even imagine would be possible."

"There have been some hard times too."

"But even the hard things have been good. Good growing times. Larry, would you dice up this ham?"

Larry went to work. "Hey, Bill."

"What?"

"Mother's Day is coming up soon. You know, we've been meeting all this time, and I don't know anything about your parents."

Bill leaned back against the counter and glanced around the room. Then he left the kitchen for a moment and came back with a framed photo. The two men carried their breakfast plates out to the table on the patio.

"This is them about ten years ago," Bill said. *"My dad passed away five years ago. My mom's still alive. She's in a retirement community in Wisconsin."* He paused again. *"Why do you bring it up?"*

"Well, it seems like we've talked about everything under the sun, and I hadn't heard you say a word about your parents. Is there a reason you're so quiet about it?"

Bill looked uncomfortable. *"I suppose just saying, 'I don't want to talk about it,' won't work with you, huh?"*

Larry set his knife down and gave Bill his full attention. *"If you really don't want to talk about it, that's okay,"* Larry said. *"But every time we've gotten close to talking about our past, family and things like that, you clam up."*

Bill sighed. *"I've never had a good relationship with my mom,"* he said. *"I haven't even talked with her for over a year now. When my dad died, I felt I lost the only parent who really loved me."*

"So you don't think your mom loves you?"

"If she does, she sure has a hard time showing it. All my life I've gotten nothing but criticism from her. She always

sees what was left undone, never what was done. And she always points out how it could have been done a little bit better. She's just so negative and controlling.

"On her last visit, she was still telling me how much sugar to put on my cereal in the morning. Imagine, at my age! She'll try to make me change my clothes if she doesn't think what I have on is appropriate. She's basically a pain in the neck.

"And she treats Diane like dirt, like she doesn't respect her as the mother of our kids and as the great woman she is. Classic mother-in-law syndrome. So it's easier for me right now just to ignore her."

"How old is she?"

"Sixty-eight, I think."

Larry thought for a second and then said, "Bill, one of your great gifts that I've always admired is that you're a peacemaker. It's like that verse you like in Romans: 'If it is possible, as far as it depends on you, live at peace with everyone.' "

"I know. And that's why I feel so guilty about this relationship—or lack of it. But I feel powerless to change anything. I've tried talking with her, and she says stuff like 'Don't talk to me like I'm one of your kids. I'm your mother!' End of conversation."

"Can I give you a challenge here?" asked Larry.

"I'm listening."

"Another really important verse is the one about honoring your parents."

"I hate that verse."

They laughed.

"But it's a verse with a promise. It basically says that if you reach out and honor your mom unconditionally, you will be blessed. 'As far as it depends on you'—that's the challenge."

"So what do you think I should do?"

"Well, maybe you could think about your mom's positive traits. List anything good that you've learned from her, any wisdom or character qualities, anything passed on in the genes that has proven to be a blessing to you."

Bill's face turned thoughtful. "You know, right away I think about how creative she is. She is artistic and kind of off-the-wall. And those are things people say they appreciate in me, things that have made me a good teacher. I never thought about that. My dad was not creative at all; all that came from my mom's side."

"Say, are you going to send your mom a Mother's Day card?"

"Haven't thought about it. Diane usually does that. Why?"

"That's a small thing you could do that wouldn't be too hard. And you could tell her some of the things you appreciate about her and thank her for them."

Bill nodded. "Larry, that's the first idea anybody has given me that could help this relationship. It feels like God is at work here. There are things she did for me at key points in my life that helped me get where I am today. I could mention those things too."

"Do you mind if I hold you accountable to writing your mom for Mother's Day?"

"Mind?" Bill chuckled. "This is an accountability relationship, isn't it?"

In any good and growing relationship it will be necessary at times to confront. Proverbs 27:17 says, "As iron sharpens iron, so one man sharpens another." Learning to sharpen one another through loving confrontation is one of the more mature skills a Christian man needs to develop if he is going to sustain and deepen an accountability relationship over time.

REASONS FOR LOVING CONFRONTATION

There are a number of reasons why we might have to lovingly confront a friend or why we ourselves might need to be confronted. First, as I have said before in this book, it is certainly true that "the heart is deceitful above all things" (Jer 17:9). We will do our best to be honest with each other, but we will still often be rationalizing our behaviors or living in denial. Remember, we rationalize when we try to give acceptable reasons for unacceptable thoughts, feelings and behaviors. And we are in denial when we refuse to acknowledge those unacceptable thoughts, feelings and behaviors. When we believe that either of these things—rationalizing or denying—might be occurring in our friend's life, then it is time for some loving confrontation.

I'll give you a hypothetical situation. You pick up negative information about your partner from some other source. For example, the grapevine could be saying that your friend acted unethically in a business deal. You don't know whether the report is true or not, but you have to bring it up with your partner. If you just let the situation go, the rumors will continue to spread and will hurt your friend. If he has acted badly, then you can encourage him to take responsibility for his unwise choice. If he has done nothing wrong, then you can help by telling others the truth when you hear the accusation being passed around. A situation like this calls for loving confrontation.

Sometimes, too, we just need to fine-tune each other. For instance, a personality trait in your friend may be causing him to harm his associates or family. I'm not talking here about a sinful behavior but about some idiosyncrasy or area for growth.

One of my friends had the habit of dominating the discussion in small-group settings. I observed it for a while and felt uncomfortable about it. Often the quieter men in the group looked like they might have something to bring to the conversation, but Jerry would always beat them to the punch, and once he started talking, he had a hard time knowing how to bring what he was saying to a close.

I met with him one day and began by telling him that I believed he had much to offer in biblical knowledge and awareness. Then I shared with him what I was observing regarding the other men in the group who couldn't contribute because Jerry was always talking. He accepted the Scripture I shared with him about being quick to listen and slow to speak.

Jerry felt assured that it wasn't what he said that was the problem. It was just that when there are twelve men in a group, every man needs to ask himself before he speaks, *Is what I'm about to say necessary to the discussion?* And if it is, then he should ask, *How can I say this briefly?* I watched Jerry put the advice into practice, and the group experience became richer as others began sharing freely and Jerry started listening to and affirming others' contributions more.

Another reason we may need to confront is that we sense a change for the worse in the way another man is relating with us. If for no apparent reason there is suddenly a sense of distance in the relationship, someone needs to bring it up. Why this change? Fight the temptation to let what appears to be a "little thing" fester until it causes deterioration in the friendship. Jump right on it and see if something needs to be set right.

Finally, when we observe sin in the life of a brother, we need to confront him. James 5:20 says, "Remember this: Whoever turns a sinner from the error of his way will save him from death and cover over a multitude of sins."

As hard as it is to confront, it is nevertheless one of

the most loving things we can do. And it is the best thing for a growing relationship if the intervention is given and received in the right spirit.

Faithful are the wounds of a friend;
   but the kisses of an enemy are deceitful.
(Prov 27:6 KJV)

If we don't confront when confrontation is called for, we cross over into the enemy camp.

PRINCIPLES FOR LOVING CONFRONTATION

The best help on sensitive confrontation comes from Galatians 6:1-2: "Brothers, if someone is caught in a sin, you who are spiritual should restore him gently. But watch yourself, or you also may be tempted. Carry each other's burdens, and in this way you will fulfill the law of Christ." Building on that word from the Bible, I'd like to share with you some insights that I have picked up over the years about how to confront lovingly.

Keep a humble attitude. Any time we feel that we need to bring loving correction into our brother's life, it is good to remember that it is always one beggar showing another beggar where to find food. I think that is why Paul used the word "gently." As we seek to restore another man to a right relationship with God, we must recognize that we ourselves are also vulnerable to sin and will need to be open to correction when our time comes. We would want to be treated gently by others, and so we should do the same.

Be a support through the change. The phrase "Carry

each other's burdens" makes it clear that our correction always works best if it occurs within a relationship where support and encouragement have already been demonstrated. This is why the accountable friendship is so important. In this relationship we have proven over time that we really do care. We have earned the right to speak the truth in love. When a man is receiving a word of criticism, he can trust that his friend has as his sole motivation to help him take another step toward maturity in Christ.

One way to check our motivation for bringing reproof is to ask ourselves whether taking the action is pleasurable or painful to us. When we find no pleasure in bringing this word to our friend, we can be fairly sure our motivations are other-centered. As children we have all been guilty of running someone else down in order to make ourselves feel better. We need to guard against this kind of immaturity when we are entering into confrontation with a friend. If we're finding any pleasure in bringing this correction, then we need to stop. Is our heart really in the right place?

Once we have opened up an important issue to a friend, we also need to commit ourselves to bringing the love, support and care that will help our brother change. There should be no hit-and-run dumping in a good accountability friendship. Helping another man come up with creative options for improvement is just as important as raising the significant issue. What are friends really for? Let's stick with our friend and walk with him in every way needed to bring about life change that would honor Christ.

Work from strengths to weaknesses. It is good to remember that problem behaviors are usually gifts being applied in excess. The man who is controlling in his leadership style may have a strong gift of organization and administration, but his problem is that he micromanages everybody close to him. In another case, a man who can't seem to be honest with his friends may be so sensitive and caring that he cannot bear the thought of saying something that might be hurtful. This gift of sensitivity and mercy gets in the way of honesty.

If you had to confront either of these men, you would start by talking about his important giftedness and then go on to show how the gift is causing the problem. In other words, begin by encouraging and then do the necessary correcting. At the end of the time, reaffirm the gift again so that you close the conversation with more affirmation. But always be strong and direct enough so that your real point will not be misunderstood.

I might say to a friend that I admire his disciplined approach to exercise. If he knows that he has been an inspiration to me in this area, it becomes easier for me to talk with him about how his disciplined attitude can slip over into perfectionism and pride, which can make others around him feel judged and inferior. He may, for instance, need to show more unconditional love to his son, who is not athletically inclined, rather than pressuring him constantly to be more like Dad. This kind of correction is received better if a person can see that the problem grows out of a talent or gift.

Speak observations, not judgments. In talking to
your friend, describe the behavior you have observed,
but hold back from stating a judgment about his motivations. Give your friend a chance to talk about what
was occurring from his point of view. That way, instead
of accusing him of something as if he were already pro-
nounced guilty, you let him have the space to explain
the observed behavior. You show that you do not already have your mind made up about the matter. This
way you don't put your friend on the defensive. Once
a person is on the defensive, he spends all of his time
thinking about his defense rather than considering
whether he really does need to make a change.

Maybe a simple example will help here. My friend
Bill has asked me to hold him accountable on his new
diet. Two days later I see him walking out of the doughnut shop, carrying a small white bag across the street to
his office. I could call him and say, "Bill, you are not living up to your promises regarding your diet. I know
you've been cheating." But statements like these would
communicate that I have already made up my mind.
Furthermore, they would put Bill in the uncomfortable
position of having to dig himself out of a hole. He
couldn't help but feel that I don't really trust him.

It would be so much better for me, the next time I
met Bill, to say with a light tone, "Are you still trying
to diet? I wondered about it when I saw you leave the
doughnut shop the other day." This way Bill would
feel less pressured and would have the space to say,
"Thanks for keeping your eye on me. But it was the

first Thursday of the month—my turn to bring the doughnuts to staff meeting. I stayed completely away from them, though. Scout's honor! I was proud of myself."

By withholding judgment about motives, you show your partner that you trust him and always think the best of him rather than the worst.

Pray before correcting. One last thought here. It is important to remember that God might be giving us discernment about our partner's life, not so that we will rush in and correct him, but rather so that we may pray for him. Often our prayer will actually bring about change before we even say a word. I've had the experience many times of praying about when and how to bring up something with a friend, and then the friend has come to me and said, "There's something that I really need to talk with you about." I was worried about how to broach the subject, but God brought the person right to me to talk about the problem!

Also, many times when I'm in prayer for a friend, God will let me know that I am not to get involved just then. Yes, I see something that needs to be set right, but God has his plan for getting it done and I'm not included in it at this point, except to pray. Sometimes we push our way in and interrupt something God is bringing to completion in a way we may not have even imagined was possible. God's timing is everything in these matters. If we take the time to bathe situations in prayer, God is able to let us know whether he wants us to intervene now, to wait or to continue to pray.

HOW DO YOU RESPOND
WHEN YOU ARE CONFRONTED?

If you believe that the goal of your Christian life is to
grow to full maturity in Christ, then you will necessar-
ily choose to have a teachable spirit. Even the humbling experience of receiving reproof from another
person is part of God's plan for our growth. Humility
is the most desirable character quality we can have as
Christian men. The Lord wants us to grow in humility
and dependence on him. There should be no room in
us for pride that refuses to consider constructive criticism from others.

I'll never forget the great attitude of a friend of mine
who worked with me some years ago. Sometimes people would come in and deliver criticism to him. When
the critic was done, my friend would say something
like, "Thank you for that. That's something I really
needed to hear. It sounds like I have some real growing
to do in this area." Then he would share what he
planned to do about it as well some other related things
he was already working on. His gracious response was
disarming to those who were used to bringing criticism
and having the one receiving it respond with anger,
hurt or defensiveness.

Welcome constructive criticism. Ask God to search
you with this information. If it is important for you to
pay attention to, you will begin to see it tie in with
other areas of struggle. Recent experiences you may
not have understood very well will suddenly be illu-
mined by heavenly wisdom. God will show you some-

thing about yourself that can lead to greater understanding and new growth.

I recently went through a difficult time with a church committee that was split on which candidate to hire for a staff position. I was certain that I knew what the right decision was. We had been searching for a long time, and I had become exhausted with the process. This added to the tension that particular evening when I found myself pushing too hard. A good friend who was also on that committee spent nearly two hours with me the next day. I appreciated his insight and his listening skills. But as I reviewed what had happened in this particular case, I started seeing a pattern in my behavior that I had not seen so clearly before.

I believe those who know me would characterize me in most situations as sensitive, patient and good at listening. What I saw in this circumstance, however, was how differently I can respond when the stakes are higher and it looks like I might not get my way. In that meeting I became defensive, controlling and intensely persuasive in my use of language.

In the weeks following, as I prayed and journaled about this, God brought a couple of difficult relationships to mind. The word that kept coming into my mind was *control*. I started seeing that my tendency to assert control when I became worried about an outcome was at the heart of some of my relationship problems. The trouble lay with me, not the others. I needed to learn how better to stay in process with people to seek God's will together rather than to assert myself, running over people or trying to manipulate them. I've had to go back and do some apologizing. It's been humbling, but it's right and good. This is how God works in our lives to bring about significant shifts in the makeup of our complex personalities.

One of the prices we pay when we are growing into leadership as Christian men is that we need to be increasingly accountable. That means that we are prayerfully open to constructive criticism that can help us grow toward greater maturity in Christ.

FOR REFLECTION OR DISCUSSION

1. Which of the principles of loving confrontation will help you to feel more confident the next time you need to confront a friend? Why?

2. In what ways do we earn the right to speak frankly and openly in an accountability friendship?

3. How do you typically respond to constructive criticism? What ideas from this chapter do you think will help you to be more teachable in the future?

4. What do you see as the major benefits of being able to receive constructive criticism? What are some important things you've learned in the past that came through relationships with others who cared enough to confront you?

7

PARTNERS IN PRAYER

IT WAS A GRAY, OVERCAST MORNING when Bill arrived at the coffee shop. Larry's disposition seemed to Bill to be overcast as well.

"So, Larry, how are you holding up?" Bill asked cautiously. "I know how disappointed you were about being passed over for the promotion."

"I'm still hurting over it. My family is still hurting over it. And there are a couple of people from work involved that I'm having a real hard time loving right now."

Bill put his arm around Larry's shoulder and said, "I've been praying for you every day about this."

"Thanks," Larry said as both men sat down. "Do you mind me asking what you've prayed for?"

"Well, basically that God would speak to you so directly on this that you would have the confidence to trust him in it and get past it. And I've prayed that this disappointment wouldn't color your whole work situation."

Larry pulled his journal out of his briefcase. "I had a conversation with God yesterday, or I should say, he had a conversation with me. It was pretty powerful. Can I read this to you?"

"Sure."

"Here goes." Larry paged through his journal and came to a particular passage. *"You have to understand that I was really grousing with the Lord about this all week. Dumping on him. I have down here all my feelings about the way the decision was made, how wrong it was. I couldn't stop thinking about the conversation with the boss and how many things he had just missed. And then I kept going over how badly I was treated after all these years at the company: the lack of communication, the distancing I felt, all of that.*

"But then I wrote, 'This is BIG. Now GOD speaks to me.' And I'm serious. He just broke through, and I kept writing. First he gave me Romans 8:28, that all things work together for good for those who love him and are called according to his purpose.

"A sense of peace and comfort flooded in. I realized deep down that God is sovereign. He even let me know right then that he was protecting me.

"I also wrote that I know from past experiences that God is already using this for my best, to grow and stretch me and develop my character. Then he actually said this—I kid you not—'Larry, be thankful in all things. You can because I will work them out to your benefit, even if it's not what you expected. Let go of what you want and let me do what's best for you!'"

"That's awesome, Larry."

"I know, but there's even more. God asked me a question then. I wrote it down. 'Will you serve me with your life even if you don't get what you want?' I stopped and prayed for a moment, then I wrote, 'YES, but it's hard!'

"Then this came from God: 'Now, you need to ask forgiveness for not appreciating what you have—the blessings I pour out on you and your family every day.'

"I wrote, 'I'm sorry, Lord. I'm still so incredibly selfish. I feel terrible right now for how much I have been focused on what I don't have rather than what I do have. Lord, if everything in the world is stripped away, I still have you. And you're the best. Thanks for showing me that!' "

"Larry, what a tremendous time you had with God."

"I know. I feel like I have a lot of hurt to work through yet . . ."

"But to have God speak so straight to you in prayer must give you the confidence that he really knows what's going on, that he's going to do the best for you, whether it's what you thought you wanted or not."

Larry's smile lit up his face. *"I can't thank you enough for praying for me,"* he said. *"God was really answering your prayers for me."*

"It's a privilege. This has been so good. Can I pray for you right now?"

"Sure."

Bill reached across the table and clasped hands with Larry. *"Lord God,"* Bill began, *"my brother here has had a really tough week. But you are a good God even when times are tough. Thank you that you made yourself known to him, that you are with him even when he faces challenges. I'm so grateful for the man you're making him to be and for his friendship in my life. We stand together here, and I pray on his behalf that you would renew his spirit and restore his soul. I pray that you will continue to speak to him, that your Holy Spirit would continue to guide him and that above all else he would know the height and depth of your love for him. In Jesus' name, amen."*

Larry looked up, his eyes watering a bit. "Thanks, Bill."

"I'm so glad to know you, Larry, and to be counted as one of your friends."

Our prayer life will make a difference in how we interact with a Christian friend in three primary areas.

First, in prayer we experience God as our Father who knows us intimately and loves us unconditionally. Our Father most effectively communicates his love to us through prayer. The most important thing we can offer anyone else in a shared relationship under God is unconditional love. We can't love another person in this powerful way unless we ourselves know the unconditional love of God. And if we have been loved generously, we will have the same generous love to share with a hurting friend.

The second important aspect that prayer brings to our relationship with a friend is discernment. God speaks to us in prayer. He reveals his own nature in marvelous and helpful ways. We can share these insights with a friend when appropriate and fitting. God will also speak to us about our friend's needs as well as things we need to see and learn about ourselves that might help or hinder the accountable relationship. So it is important to be learning more all the time about how to hear God better.

Third, we understand from Scripture that God is eager to hear from us in prayer. He considers our heartfelt requests according to his will for our lives and the lives of those for whom we pray. In Job 16:20-21 we read, "My intercessor is my friend as my eyes pour out tears to God; on behalf of a man he pleads with God as a man pleads for his friend." In our accountable relationship with a friend we will be bringing each other's needs before the Lord on a regular basis through intercessory prayer.

It is therefore necessary for us to have a living relationship with the Lord if we want to pass on Christ's love and heavenly wisdom to our friend. Our prayers will also often be the catalyst for needed change. Over time we experience often in a Christian friendship the wonderful reality of answered prayer. Our faith in the faithfulness of God grows as we watch God work in each other's lives.

Our prayer relationship with the Father is the source of everything for an accountable relationship that is filled with life.

PRAYER IS A GIFT FROM GOD

The mere fact that the possibility of prayer exists for us

as believers is powerful proof that God is highly motivated to spend time with us. It is almost as if he is ob-
sessed with love for us. Catherine of Genoa, one of the
great Christian mystics, told of an experience she had
during which God informed her that if she really knew
the full extent of his love, it would kill her.

Our Father wants to reveal himself to us. He wants
us to know him, even the deeper things, by the Spirit (1
Cor 2:10). And he is eager to see how we will respond
when he initiates relationship with us. That is what the
practice of prayer really is. Prayer is in essence our
growing willingness to receive more of the presence of
God. James promised, "Come near to God and he will
come near to you" (Jas 4:8).

Prayer is a love gift from God. Yet for too many
years I just didn't understand that. I carried confused
and mistaken notions about prayer. I agreed with the
Westminster Catechism that the chief aim of life is to
glorify God and enjoy him forever. But then why was it
that prayer—the intimate way God has provided for
me to enjoy him—had become burdensome and sometimes even boring to me?

I remember feeling especially guilty about my
struggles with intercessory prayer (praying for the
needs of others). At the beginning of any week I
might have two or three prayer requests jotted down
in my journal. By Thursday it might have grown to
ten or twenty. By then my praying felt like a rote and
meaningless exercise. I was merely going through the
motions. I persisted in it dutifully, but the experience

felt empty, devoid of the Spirit of God.

A friend I was talking to about my struggle asked me to describe my best experiences of closeness with God. I thought immediately about personal worship times—playing piano and singing my favorite praise and worship songs with all my heart. I also mentioned my more reflective times, reading Scripture and praying through the verses. At these times I felt connected with God. My prayers were most real when I was not trying to tell God anything or ask him for anything. My best times were when I was just with God and he was with me, in quietness.

My friend asked me how often I was enjoying these times with God. I admitted that these really close times with God were infrequent. I felt so guilty about what I considered to be my failure in intercessory prayer that I spent all my time there, trying desperately to do better, dutifully reading my long lists of requests out loud toward my office ceiling. At that point my wise friend said, "Tom, pray as you can, not as you can't. It is the first rule of prayer."

That suggestion began revolutionizing my relationship with God. I started spending more time at the piano, singing praise and worship songs, attending to the meaning of the lyrics, pausing often to listen to God's stirrings in my heart and mind. I spent more time praying through Scripture. And I spent much more time just sitting quietly before the Lord, sensing his presence and letting him pour his love into my heart. The joy was returning.

Prayer is a gift from God for our enjoyment of him. My mistake was that I had come to believe it was my responsibility to make my prayer life fruitful. I realize now that I have no power to make prayer become anything. God is the initiator, center and source of all that happens in prayer. If we feel responsible for the effectiveness of our prayer life, it will paralyze us. Letting go of the notion that we have the power to make or break our prayer lives is a doorway to freedom.

This paradigm shift in my understanding and practice of prayer revitalized my intercessory prayers. I might be singing a favorite praise song, and the lyrics would remind me of someone's personal need. I would stop and pray for that person. The same thing would happen as I prayed through Scripture. People and issues would come to mind, and I would attend to them in prayer. I interceded more meaningfully than before because my prayer came from a sense of call—God was calling my attention to this need in the midst of prayer.

Prayer is an invitation from God to share in the riches of his life and love, his grace and freedom, his joy. God's invitation to you is personal and individual. There is no set style or method that you must follow to have a prayer relationship with your Father. Every authentic believer has his or her own individual manner of responding to God's call to walk in relationship with him. Your personal prayer life will be as unique as your calling and giftedness in serving God. The more natural you will be in responding to God in your personality style, the more you will grow in your relationship with him.

Pray as you can, not as you can't. Don't force yourself to pray in ways that do not work for you just because someone else has success in that style. Let God lead you in developing your prayer life in ways that are fitting for you.

Prayer at its best comes by realizing more fully each day God's presence and intimate involvement in every aspect of our lives—our joys, our depressions, our pains, our promises, our relationships, our work, our studies, our worship, our family lives, our play. To pray is to recognize God's initiating activity in all of life, from the most spiritually charged moments to the most ordinary day-to-day activities. When Jesus chose the bread and wine to be his body and blood to us, he chose the most ordinary elements of human existence and promised he would be present there. Every aspect of who we are and what we do is sacramental—he is present in it all.

Our awareness of God's presence in all of life, and our response to his initiating love, are the essence of the life of prayer. It is this continually expanding dialogue with God that Paul must have had in mind when he said we can "pray without ceasing" (1 Thess 5:17 KJV).

GOD'S UNCONDITIONAL LOVE RECEIVED IN PRAYER

A vital prayer life is necessary for each of the members of an accountable relationship. If we do not know and experience the Lord's life and unconditional love, then we have nothing of real value to pass on to anyone else. Knowing God's love well enough to give it away starts with our prayer relationship with our Father.

When we risk honesty with God about our weakness, our dryness, our deep sinfulness, we come to know God as he really is—a God of love. God is present at all times in our lives as unconditional love. The more honest we are with God in prayer, the more deeply we will experience God's love. If God would allow his beloved Son to die for us while we were enemies of grace, how much more will he be pleased to show his love to us now that we are his friends, even his own children?

We learn through our intimate prayer journey that we do not need to prove anything to God, nor could we if we wanted to. We cannot bargain with him, blackmail him or coerce him. We cannot negotiate for or purchase God's love. When we come repeatedly to our Father in openness about our frailties, we find that he loves us. This astonishes us—and makes us profoundly thankful.

God shows us his goodness when we are in our deepest need. He heals the pain of our sinful choices with his love and grace. He gives us a new start in him. All he looks for is humility. Living in that posture in prayer, we receive his mercy. In honest prayer we touch his undeserved and unreserved love.

When Jesus knew about the sin of his disciples, even that one of them would betray him, how did he respond? He stripped and knelt before them, serving them in love as he washed their feet. God is like that. We hurt God with our sinful choices, often ignoring him or letting ourselves get wrapped up in the blessings and forgetting the One who gives them. But when we turn to God, convicted in our sin, he serves us with another course of his unconditional love and forgiveness.

Christ's relationship to the hurting and the lost was always a ministry of love. You have this same sort of ministry with your friend, and he has this ministry of Christ in your life. You both know how to love because Christ first loved you (1 Jn 4:19). Paul wrote, "Now about brotherly love we do not need to write to you, for you yourselves have been taught by God to love each other" (1 Thess 4:9). And you learn this love most intimately in your honest interactions with God in prayer.

There ought to be ways that men can say to one another in an accountable friendship that there is nothing either one could ever do that would separate him from his friend's love. Love may have to be tough sometimes, but it is always unconditional if its true source is God. That's what we learn from the love of our Father. And again, we learn it best by experiencing God's love poured out generously on us as we enter the Father's presence in prayer.

PRAYER FOR DISCERNMENT

In prayer we develop an ear for God's voice and an eye for noticing God in the interaction we share with a friend. Discernment is having a sense from the Holy Spirit regarding whether our discussions are heading toward a dead end or whether we are nearing a place where a little more digging will produce gold.

It is important to be in a prayerful attitude while listening to each other. I sometimes refer to this experience as listening in surround sound. We attend to our friend's sharing while at the same time paying attention to what is going on inside our own heart, listening there for God to tell us something he wants us to pursue.

A prayerful attitude during discussions will result in our noticing things that we might have missed if we had not asked God to lead us. As we grow in our confidence to act on promptings of the Holy Spirit, our ear for God is sensitized.

These prayerful listening skills can be learned, although some people do have special gifts in this area. If you are interested in more study on this topic, one good book is *The Art of Christian Listening* by Thomas N. Hart. My experience has been that anyone who sincerely seeks the Lord's leading in this kind of mutual discipling experiment will not be disappointed. God is eager to be known and heard.

This is an area where one friend can help another fine-tune his spiritual intuitions. I have rarely said "Thus saith the Lord!" in my relationship with a Christian friend. Normally I express what I am sensing more tentatively, like "Jim, while you were telling me that story about your son, I had a sense that there was a story about you and your father somewhere in the background." That gives Jim the opportunity to consider whether this prompting to go deeper is from the Lord. Such an approach is one way we can help each other grow in our ability to discern the voice of God from other voices that might arise within us.

As we spend time with each other and with God in

prayer, God will help us to discern the true source of something that comes up in discussion. God will guide us by his Spirit to know the meanings of those things that gather importance as we grow our friendship. We will come to understand why God might surface a particular item at this time. This helps us answer the question "Now that we've heard this from God, what are we supposed to do about it?"

That is the essence of the accountable relationship. We are all about hearing a true word from God, interpreting the meaning of it for us and deciding what to do about it. This process is at the heart of all authentic Christian growth.

HEARING GOD'S VOICE

Through the ages God has spoken to his people through his written Word; by prophetic utterance; in dramatic actions and lived-out parables; through successes or failures in life's projects; by the casting of lots, personal intuitions, and feelings of peace or discontentment; and through direct communication, dreams, answered prayers, unanswered prayers (which are really answers in disguise), fleeces, and the responses of other believers to a thought or vision. God might use any of these methods today to help us discern his will for ourselves or for our friend. Having such experiences, however, will still require us to exercise spiritual discernment in deciding whether the source of the experience is the Lord. And if we gain confidence that the experience really is from the Lord, then discernment is needed again to properly interpret the wisdom and apply it to our lives.

I know of no manual for learning to hear God and discern his will in this way. Our time spent in God's Word, however, creates a backdrop of truth that helps us to spiritually sift our experiences. Our regular diet of communication with God refines our sensitivity to God's voice among the many other voices that might arise within us. Jesus said, "My sheep recognize my voice" (Jn 10:27 *The Message*).

If we want to be men who are growing in our ability to hear the Lord, then we should be engaged in the regular rhythms of prayer, Bible reading and study, self-reflection, and self-examination. Also, we should be open to testing our spiritual intuitions with other believers. After all, we grow in the skill of hearing God by submitting our more subjective awarenesses to the counsel of other well-grounded Christian people. If we decide that we are so competent at discerning the Lord's will that we don't need to consult others in the testing of the spirits, we will become dangerous.

Earlier in my walk with the Lord my confidence in counseling and discipling rested mainly on the teachings of Scripture. Then as I grew in Christ, there were times when I would have intuitions about a situation or a person. At first I dismissed them, afraid of the subjectivity of these personal feelings. But as time went on, I noticed my intuitions would often be proved true by events. Then I wondered if I might have failed God and others by not having the confidence to act on these leadings from the Lord.

So I decided to test my intuitions and became bolder in acting on them. The result is that God has blessed me with growing sensitivity and confidence in my ability to hear his voice. I am now much more open to accepting the wide variety of ways God may choose to speak into my life or into the lives of others through me. I still have much to learn about hearing God, but I am thankful for his persistence in developing my ability to notice his fingerprints on insights and intuitions I may have.

You can make gaining spiritual intuition a point of prayer for yourself and your partner. Ask the Lord daily for greater spiritual discernment and a growing confidence that he will speak. Ask him to bless both of you with ears to hear him and eyes to see him. If you and your accountability partner want to grow in spiritual sensitivity, and if your motivation is to more fruitfully serve God and love others, God will answer your prayer.

INTERCESSORY PRAYER

Prayer is the greatest power we have to influence the course of our lives and the lives of others.

Almost everywhere we turn in the letters of Paul we find him telling the churches how he was praying for them. For instance, Paul prayed that God would enlighten the Ephesians to the true hope they had, that they would live in the riches of their inheritance and that they would understand fully that Christ's resurrection power was available to them (Eph 1:15-21).

Paul was also not shy about asking for prayer for himself. Near the end of Ephesians 6, for example, he asks the church to pray that he would use the right words in sharing the gospel with others. But I think the full extent of Paul's faith in intercessory prayer can be seen in 1 Timothy 2:1-2, where he writes, "I urge . . . that requests, prayers, intercession and thanksgiving be made for everyone—for kings and all those in authority." The message is plain: prayer has the power to influence the course of people's lives and world events.

One of Jesus' priorities was the ministry of intercessory prayer. In John 17 he says to the Father, "I pray for them. I am not praying for the world, but for those you have given me" (v. 9). The Bible teaches us that intercessory prayer is Jesus' primary ministry to this day. "Christ Jesus, who died—more than that, who was raised to life—is at the right hand of God and is also interceding for us" (Rom 8:34).

Certainly, if this heavenly power to bring about change is truly available to us, we will want to be praying daily for our friend. We will pray about the important issues that surface in our mutual sharing. We will bring before the Father specific requests our friend shares with us, trusting God to act according to his sovereign will. And when the situation is so difficult that we do not even know how to pray, we can trust that "the Spirit himself intercedes for us with groans that words cannot express" (Rom 8:26).

I know when people are praying for me. At such times I have a wonderful sense of being carried along by the Spirit and experiencing his peace. Often I have an awareness of being guided or having wisdom beyond what I could naturally bring to a situation. It is a wonderful gift to be regularly lifting others up before the Lord in prayer.

In my men's group it is a blessing each week to close our time with the sharing of prayer requests. This morning one man shared that his sister is in an abusive marriage. Another man is contemplating taking a board position at a Christian school. A third man's purchase of a new home had hit some road bumps. I asked for prayer for a son who is struggling with a powerful addiction. With united hearts we bring the common things of life before the Lord. Could there be any more practical or purposeful way to express our love for one another?

It's helpful to remember there are some general things we can always pray for a friend. We can pray that God will lead him into a greater understanding of the Lord's will for his life. Paul prayed for the Colossians that God would fill them with the "knowledge of his will through all spiritual wisdom and understanding" (Col 1:9). We can always pray as well that our partner will have the courage to act obediently when he knows the will of the Lord. In the next verse Paul prays that the church will "live a life worthy of the Lord and may please him in every way: bearing fruit in every good work" (v. 10). Then Paul goes on to pray that the church will be "strengthened with all power according to his glorious might" (v. 11). We too can always pray for spiritual power for our accountable friend.

A MATURING PRAYER FOCUS

Maturing in our prayer life means maturing in our relationship with God. As we grow in the Lord, we will find that we ask less frequently for material blessings and that we're not as concerned about God's making life smooth and hassle free for us. We will be less preoccupied with ourselves and our attention will shift dramatically to the majesty and goodness of God.

The center of our life with God is not a religious technique fueled by personal discipline and a sense of duty. It is a growing fascination with the awesome and glorious character of God the Father as he reveals himself more fully to us. There is no end to the marvelous journey of discovery to know him better.

Prayer contains all the elements of an absorbing and rewarding mutual friendship. It is a friendship with the One who will never let us down or disappoint us in his love. We were created to enjoy this fellowship; it is our reason for existence. And prayer is how we open ourselves to God's initiating love and learn to give ourselves more completely to the One who wants to give himself completely to us.

In an accountable relationship with a good friend, we can encourage one another to be responsive to God in prayer. It is one of the areas we will want to regularly report on to each other. We will find ourselves talking about God's wisdom delivered to us in prayer, how his guidance applies perfectly to a situation that had been confusing or frustrating to us. We will exalt together the goodness of God as he brings his love and mercy into our midst.

How wonderful it is to celebrate the fact that God is with us and relishes intimate dialogue with us, his close friends!

FOR REFLECTION OR DISCUSSION

1. In your own words, summarize the three areas the author highlights as ways prayer will make a difference in your relationship with an accountable friend.

2. What would it mean for you to pray as you can and not as you can't?

3. What major obstacles do you think stand in the way of men having a more meaningful prayer relationship with God?

4. Describe your prayer journey with God from your first attempts to talk with him up to the present time. After reading this chapter, is there anything that you think God might want you to be doing differently in your prayer life?

5. How do you see God working in your life to create in you a growing sensitivity to his voice?

6. How has God answered the prayers you have prayed for others? How important do you believe it is for you and your accountability partner to regularly pray for each other?

8   GETTING STARTED

Dave sat down in the booth across from Bill and Larry. "Do you guys always meet here? For doughnuts?"

"No," Larry said. "Sometimes we go for pancakes and sausage."

"Or bagels and cream cheese at the place down the street," Bill added.

"What about your arteries?" Dave asked, raising an eyebrow.

"So far, so good," Bill said. And then with a guilty laugh, "It's only once a week."

"You can get a veggie omelet with EggBeaters over at Harriet's. If you decide to meet with us, we'll go there once in a while, I promise." Larry put his hand over his heart.

"I don't know if I'll be able to survive you two," Dave said, joking. "But anyway, tell me what this is all about."

"Well," Bill began, "we've both been praying for weeks about adding someone to our weekly meeting time. No pressure here, but your name came to Larry and to me separately. We thought maybe God was putting you on our minds. So we want to tell you what we do and then see if you'd be interested in joining us."

"It was over a year ago," Larry said, "that I approached Bill about meeting together. I told him then that I really didn't have any close friends—I mean really close. I had let life's busyness squeeze out something that I've come to believe now, more than ever, is absolutely essential. In this past year of meeting with Bill, I have grown more than I did in the previous ten years. These times of study, prayer and holding one another accountable are highlights of my week, every week."

"I totally agree," Bill jumped in. "And we really wouldn't have to eat anything. I was just kidding about that. When we finish up together, I often have half my food on my plate yet. These times are that stimulating to me.

"And I have learned in this past year what a real friendship is. We've been through a lot of highs and lows together, but we've found the Lord in it all. A best friend will help you see the Lord in everything. We also get the families together for fun. It's been great."

"Being single, that sounds pretty good to me," Dave said. "My family is all upstate. I'd enjoy a home-cooked meal or good barbecue once in a while."

"You'd be welcome," Larry said. "But we don't do all family things. We've got our monthly men's night out too. Testosterone movies and sports. It's a lot of fun."

"Basically, Dave," Bill said, "it's been so good for Larry and me that we knew we had to open this up to at least one other guy. And later maybe more."

"Tell me what you do when you meet," Dave said. "What's it all about?"

Both Larry and Bill had their mouths full at the same time. It was quiet for half a minute. All three men laughed.

Then Larry said, "We work hard on making this a safe and confidential meeting. Learning each week how to be more honest and open with each other. Digging around in the places where we know we need to grow in the Lord."

"It's a good mix of fun and serious, life-changing stuff," Bill said. "I walk away from every meeting having something new to sink my teeth into. When things are going good, I have another guy to share it with. When things stink, I don't have to go through it alone. I know that Larry will pray for me every day.

"Dave, if this even sounds a little bit interesting to you, we'd like to talk with you more about it next week. We've got some basic ground rules to share. We made these covenants with one another about a year ago, and it would be good for us to look at them again anyway," Bill continued.

"And you could pray about it this week and think about it. Come next week with more questions, anything you can think of," Larry said.

"And if you did decide to try meeting with us, then we could set up, like, a three-month period just for you to try it. If it's not something that's working for you, no hard feelings. It won't change anything between us."

"We know there has to be a chemistry to something like this," Larry added. "We're glad to have you join us, even just to try it out for a while and see how it fits."

"I don't see how I could turn that down," Dave said. "I'm

not traveling as much as I used to, so I'm pretty sure about my availability. I'll pray this week. Where do you gluttons want to meet next week?"

"How about pancakes and sausages?" Bill said, rubbing the part of his stomach that stuck out over his belt.

The three men got up, shook hands and committed to the following week's meeting at the pancake house.

As you have been reading this book, you have probably been asking God who you might invite into a relationship of friendship and accountability. You may already have sensed a certain chemistry developing between you and another Christian man. Or as you read through the qualities to look for in a Christian friend in chapter three, you may have realized there were men in your web of relationships who meet the qualifications. But if you aren't sure of anyone yet, then begin now to ask God who you should approach about being in an accountable relationship.

GETTING TO KNOW EACH OTHER

Once you have identified a particular man, arrange a meeting time to tell him why you believe entering into a friendship with another Christian man can help you to be more honest and responsive to God. Don't hold back in telling the other man why you believe God has identified him as a possible candidate for friendship and accountability. If you enjoy spending time with him and admire some of the qualities you see in him, tell him about those things.

If the other man is open to discussing the idea further, offer him this book to look through for a week or two while both of you pray for God's guidance about whether you should proceed. Lending your potential partner the book will help him to have a better idea of your hopes and expectations for the relationship.

At this first meeting you should also share your thoughts about how often you would meet as well as any other particulars that would help the other man decide whether he ought to take this important step. Sharing your hopes for what you would like to gain in the relationship helps the other man to begin to envision what he might gain as well.

The man you approach may not be ready to re-arrange his priorities to accommodate spending adequate time with you. I approached a man once and asked him to consider going deeper with me in friendship. I knew that he liked me just as much as I liked him, but when I told him the time commitment I thought would be required, he turned me down. He said he could not take any more time from his family and business at that stage in his life. I understood, even though I was disappointed. A couple of years later, however, when his circumstances changed, we began spending more time together. To this day we remain good friends.

The person you approach may want the same things you do but just not be able to take the step now. You don't want your potential partner to enter into a demanding relationship like this casually. If both partners are not committed from the start, you will not get what you're hoping for from the relationship.

If, however, after a couple of weeks you both feel good about talking further and continuing to meet, you might create a trial period of meetings to see how things go. You could decide, for instance, to meet once a week for ten weeks.

Your first meeting could be a time to get to know one another better. Sharing the most significant points in your individual spiritual journeys would be a good place to begin. How did each of you come to know Jesus? What have been some of your most important growth experiences in the Lord since that time?

Then weeks two through ten might focus on the content of this book. The discussion questions provided for each chapter will help you stay on track.

Week ten can also be an evaluative time when you both discuss how things are going and whether it seems right to continue. If you want to go on together, you will have to make some decisions at that point. I'll talk about this a little later in this chapter.

I recommend beginning each of these initial meetings with prayer, asking God to lead the time. He will answer that prayer. End each meeting with prayer as well, praying for items of concern in each other's lives. It is important to walk away from each shared time knowing how you can continue to support your brother in prayer between meetings.

Another weekly exercise that can help you both learn to open your lives to each other is to ask one another the following questions in order, waiting for your partner to respond fully to each question before going on to the next. Of course, you should practice good listening skills while your partner is giving his answer.

• What was one high point in your week?

• What was one low point?

• Where did you see God at work in the high point?

• Where did you see God at work in the low point?

Good accountability friends help their partners find God in every aspect of every day's experience. He is there. We just need to learn better how to see him and how to hear him.

In addition, use some of the accountability questions in appendix B each week. I've been in groups where men have shown real creativity with questions like these. One man used to ask me occasionally, "Which of these questions are you hoping I won't ask you this week?" That always made me search my soul. Another man in our small group would often ask during our closing time, "Have any of you lied in any of your answers during our time today?" That was a challenging question that often took us deeper, sometimes pointing us in a direction for beginning the next week's session.

There is one more important skill for growing the relationship, one that I believe does not come naturally for men: learn to articulate for your friend your true feelings about how you think the relationship is going. Don't be afraid to express openly the emotions you are experiencing as your relationship matures. If you have enjoyed being with your friend, tell him that.

Helpful statements can start out like this one: "What I really like and admire about you is . . ." I hope you can feel comfortable saying something so simple as "I'm thankful to have you as a friend." I have personally been deeply touched by longtime friends and study partners who have felt the freedom to give me a hug and say, "I love you, brother."

It's true that your friend may not be in the same place as you in his feelings toward the developing relationship, but that's okay. It's still important for you to be honest about how you're feeling toward him. Risk telling him how significant he is becoming in your life. That kind of honesty will grow the relationship. We need to get real with each other and move our relationships off the more shallow levels that are so typical with men.

One of the great friendships recorded in the Bible was between David and Saul's son Jonathan. These two men were real men's men, through and through. As a boy, David killed a lion and a bear and even a giant Philistine, Goliath. Jonathan was one of the great military leaders in Old Testament times. But these men were not afraid of showing real emotion in their relationship as friends. They wept with one another and expressed unashamedly their love for each other. Likewise, Christian men need to let one another know that they care about each other.

Can you talk in the language of feelings as easily as you can in the language of facts? Some of your discussions early on can open up the topic of how you both feel about men expressing honest feelings. You can ask how easy or hard it is for each of you to discuss the more personal aspects of your life with another person. These discussions can help you to get to know the other man better and understand where you would both most like to grow in these sensitive relational areas.

MAKING AN AGREEMENT TO CONTINUE

If both of you are growing in God and enjoying the relationship after ten weeks, you will then need to decide where to go next. The following areas of advice will help you think through the practical considerations of what you will do during your times together and what you are hoping to accomplish. Based on what you talk about, you might even want to create a contract to sign, although it is not necessary to be that formal.

1. Schedule your meetings. What time will you meet? For how long? Where?

2. Determine how you will manage your time together. How much time will you spend in study? In personal sharing? In asking accountability questions? In prayer?

3. Decide who will lead your meetings. Or if you are going to share the leadership, decide what that will look like.

4. If you are going to include a study time in your meetings, choose what you will study together, perhaps a portion of Scripture or a meaty Christian book.

5. Make an agreement regarding confidentiality.

6. Agree to be as honest, truthful and vulnerable as you can be about the things you share for prayer and accountability.

7. Make a covenant to pray daily for each other.

8. Select some future date to evaluate how the relationship is going and whether you want to change or add to any of these previously agreed-on arrangements.

You are now ready to begin an adventure with a friend that can bring a richness in relationship with him and with God that you may never have thought possible. You are opening your lives to God in a productive way, letting God search you and challenge you and bless you through this committed, godly friendship.

I'm excited for you because I know how much God can do in this relationship. He is truly able to do "immeasurably more than all we ask or imagine, according to his power that is at work within us" (Eph 3:20). So think about this: no matter what goal the two of you have in mind for this unique relationship, God will do much more for you! An accountable relationship like this has the potential to grow you immensely and, with your developing maturity in Christ, to expand your horizon for ministry.

When we are becoming everything we can be in God, we experience the greatest joy possible as Christian men. God begins to use us in amazing ways in his life-changing work. It doesn't get any better than this.

Fasten your seat belt and hang on. This is going to be some great ride.

FOR REFLECTION OR DISCUSSION

1. Think through the time commitment you believe would be necessary for an accountability relationship. Write it down so that when you approach another man you can spell out the commitment level as accurately as possible.

2. How will you know that the person you're approaching is right for the relationship you're seeking? Try to come to some kind of understanding of how you will make your decision, but stay open for a possible surprise from God.

3. Start practicing in your own life the daily exercise the author suggests that you do with your accountability partner. Ask yourself the following questions daily, and then prayerfully evaluate your answers.

- What was one high point in your week (or day)?
- What was one low point?
- Where did you see God at work in the high point?
- Where did you see God at work in the low point?

4. How comfortable are you with letting another man know that you care about him, even that you love him? Does this need to be an area of growth for you?

5. Do you agree with the author that an accountability relationship can produce in your life far more benefits than you can even imagine now? If so, this kind of faith will carry you through doubts and fears to a growing confidence in God's good plan for your shared life with others.

APPENDIX A
The Dark Night Experience

St. John of the Cross first wrote about the "dark night of the soul" during the mid to late 1500s. John saw that Christians would often encounter dry and difficult periods in their relationship with God. In fact, Christians throughout history have found themselves in these difficult and disorienting times. When such times happen to us, we wonder what kind of work God is doing. We experience intense spiritual and emotional pain, and when we need God the most, he seems strangely absent.

In an authentic dark night experience, though it appears to us on one level of awareness that God has left us, we have a deeper sense that this abandonment is a work of God in our lives. We know this time of painful wounding is Love at work in us. We had become too fond of leaning on some personal security—and consequently leaning away from God. But with the removal of that false security, it is good to be free again to more fully follow the one true God. We might even begin to have the courage to pray, as St. John of the Cross often prayed, "God, wound me and make me whole."

It's comforting to be able to say to ourselves or to

others that we believe this tough time is a work of God in progress, not just some random, senseless event. It is comforting to grasp by faith that God is at work, even though he may not now be present in ways that we would normally recognize. We can trust that he is getting something done in us that will lead to greater joy and peace in him. He is crucifying something that needs to die in order for us to walk more closely with him. But this death, in God, leads to resurrection and new life.

HELPING A FRIEND THROUGH THE DARK NIGHT

If your friend is entering into a "dark night," remember the following guidelines.

Be patient. The deeper changes God may be aiming at cannot occur in a few days. Sometimes these periods can last for months or for a year or more. Your primary responsibility as a good and loving friend is to be praying continually that you might hear God with your friend. You must have patience to endure what might be a prolonged time when you are shown little progress in your friend's life. Pray that you may have the eyes to see your friend's life in a new way, recognizing the different future the Lord is bringing about through this tough time of searching and renewal.

Pray long and hard before meddling. It can be agonizing to see a friend who has had a strong faith and strong self-image enter a painful period of self-doubt. Your temptation will be to try to reduce this distress by building the man up in what he was before. But this may not be what God is doing. Your friend does not need sympathy at this point, but rather the simple assurance that you will be there with him through the whole disorienting process God has him in.

Do not be too quick to draw conclusions or give theological explanations for what is happening. Fight the temptation to minimize the experience in order to make your friend feel better temporarily. This is not just some emotional hiccup but a fundamental reorganization of the spirit. Stay in the experience with your friend, as uncomfortable as it may be, and pray continually for him to experience God in whatever new way the Lord might be bringing about.

Don't pressure your friend to get involved. One of the classic responses to a dark night experience is for the person to withdraw from previous commitments and involvements. The temptation for you will be to suggest reentering activity as a solution. You may become frustrated with a friend who does not appear to be doing anything about his situation, but you need to realize that it may be the "doing more" and "trying harder" that God is wanting to eliminate from his life.

Solitude may be exactly what God wants your friend to experience. Up to this point, he may have been too busy, too results-oriented, too much in control, too propped up by supportive relationships. You don't know why God may be setting this person aside for a while, but you may do more harm than good by pressuring your friend to turn away from solitude and jump back into activity.

Be willing to be hurt. Any time a person goes

through a transition with God, he experiences grief, loss and even anger. Your friend could lash out at you, especially if you believe that God may be doing a work in him that requires you to take a different posture toward him than you have taken in the past. He might feel that you're deserting him.

Try to talk things through from the perspective of what you think God may be trying to accomplish. Address why going on as usual might hinder rather than help his progress. This is dangerous territory, but God can see you both through it. Your friend needs to know that you care and will continue to be present and available but that this new situation may be calling for a new style of relating for both of you.

Jesus Christ came to earth and experienced a dark night like no other in the history of humankind—and he suffered the worst of it while separated from his Father. He suffered this for us, not so that we would never have to suffer, but so that when we do suffer, we might become more like him.

FURTHER READING

Cronk, Sandra. *Dark Night Journey: Inward Re-patterning Toward a Life Centered in God.* Wallingford, Penn.: Pendle Hill, 1991.

St. John of the Cross. *Dark Night of the Soul,* 3rd ed. Garden City, N.Y.: Image, 1959.

Matthew, Iain. *The Impact of God: Soundings from St. John of the Cross.* London: Hodder & Stoughton, 1999.

APPENDIX B
Accountability Questions

At some time during your regular meetings you and your partner (or the members of your group) will want to ask each other questions like the ones listed in this appendix to hold one another accountable. You can use these questions in a number of ways:

- You may want to ask questions randomly from the list at each of your meetings.

- Ask your friend to tell you what area he most wants to work on. Then use questions from that grouping for a while to help him concentrate on the growth he's most interested in achieving.

- Pray during the week about what question(s) to ask your friend or open up in your group. Let the Lord guide you regarding the area that needs to be addressed, even guide you to particular questions.

- Have each man come prepared with one question from the list that he has decided is the one he is most *uncomfortable* answering. This strategy will get to the heart of the matter with everybody.

- Spend your whole meeting time asking accountability questions, except for a closing time of prayer. Or do a Bible study or book study first, then turn to a couple of questions and a brief sharing time before closing in prayer.

Don't limit yourselves to the questions below. As you grow your relationship, many questions you ask will flow naturally from the needs that surface. The better you know one another, the more effective your accountable sharing time should become.

Remember the key elements of love, grace and mercy as you go into these times of in-depth sharing with each other. These questions are meant to open up areas for discussion and growth. They should not be used to batter one another. Ask the questions in a gentle manner. You might even want to read Galatians 6:1-3 at the beginning of each accountable sharing time; that passage about the fruit of the Spirit will help you maintain the right balance in your attitude toward one another.

YOUR RELATIONSHIP WITH GOD

1. When did you take time to worship God this week?
2. How much prayer time did you find this week, and was it quality time with God? Describe your prayer life this week to your partner(s).
3. Did you find adequate time to do devotional and reflective reading this week? in Scripture? in other sources?
4. How did you and your spouse meet with God together this week?
5. What did you thank God for this week?
6. What has been a struggle area for you in your devotional life this week?

7. What do you see as the number-one need to address in the coming weeks in your relationship with the Lord?

8. Do you feel that you have accomplished your spiritual aims for the week?

9. In what ways did you feel God was blessing you this week? What disappointment (if any) consumed your thoughts this week?

YOUR RELATIONSHIP WITH YOUR SPOUSE

1. What did you do this week to strengthen your relationship with your spouse?

2. How good do you think your communication with your spouse is right now? How good would your spouse say your communication is right now?

3. Did you go out this week with your wife as a couple? Did you find other significant personal time with her that was strengthening for your marriage?

4. What stresses in your marriage have the potential to distract you from being your best together? How might the stresses be relieved?

5. Are you praying regularly about your marriage?

6. How have you encouraged your spouse this week?

7. How have you spoken positively about your spouse to others this week?

8. How have you felt encouraged by your spouse this week?

9. Have you held hands, kissed each other and hugged each other this week?

10. Have you said, "I love you"?

11. Have you admitted you were wrong about something this week and asked for forgiveness?

12. What have you and your spouse done for fun recently?

13. What need would you like your spouse to meet? Have you discussed this need with your spouse?

YOUR RELATIONSHIP WITH YOUR CHILDREN

1. Have you been a good listener to your kids this week? each one?

2. Have you been able to spend *quantity* as well as *quality* time with each of your children this week? What did you do together?

3. When was the last time you attended something one of your children was taking part in (sports event, musical performance and so on)? How many such events have you missed lately? For what reasons?

4. Have you told your children that you love them and you're proud of them? each one?

5. What has been difficult for you in your relationship with any of your children this week? What have you done to resolve difficult problems?

6. Have you hurt any of your children? Have you disappointed or exasperated any of your children? If so, did you ask forgiveness?

7. Are you eating dinner together as a family?

8. Have you found time to play with your kids?

YOUR WORK LIFE

1. Have you been able to meet your personal expectations in your work this week?

2. Did you make any work-related decisions this week that lacked integrity?

3. How satisfied are you in your present work assignment? If you are dissatisfied, is the problem your work or is it your attitude?

4. How good are your work relationships? Is there anything you could do to make any of your work relationships better?

5. What is your greatest joy in your work? your biggest disappointment?

6. How did you pour yourself into your work in a creative way this week?

7. How effective were you in your use of time?

8. What area of your work is exciting to you as you launch out in a new direction?

9. How have you shared the gospel with someone at work lately?

10. Are you protecting your days off for yourself and for your family?

YOUR ATTITUDE TOWARD MONEY
AND MATERIAL THINGS

1. Did you experience any feelings of jealousy or covetousness related to material things this past week?

2. Is your giving to the Lord challenging, sacrificial and satisfying? Are you meeting your financial goals in regard to the Lord's work?

3. What personal and family goals have you made recently to help you to continue being a good steward of your finances?

4. In what specific area do you struggle in an ongoing way to be free from the control of money and things?

5. Have you struggled with greed this week?

6. Have you responded spontaneously to a surprise need in someone else's life recently?

7. Have you forgiven another's debt to you?

8. What differences in financial attitudes do you and your spouse have that could potentially create disagreements? How are you progressing in managing these differences?

YOUR CHRISTIAN BEHAVIOR

1. Have you made any decisions or taken any actions this week that compromised your integrity as a Christian?

2. Have you lied about anything?

3. Is the "you" that you project in public the real you? Where are there inconsistencies?

4. What have you done for someone else this week? How have you shown compassion and care?

5. What are you wrestling with in your thought life?

6. How have you been tempted this week? How did you respond to the temptation?

7. Did you look at a woman in the wrong way?

8. Did you put yourself in an awkward situation with any member of the opposite sex?

9. What sin has plagued you since we met last?

10. How did you lose control of your tongue this week?

How will you try to prevent this in the future?

11. How well have you treated the difficult people in your life this week?

12. Have you discussed any topic with someone of the opposite sex this week that felt inappropriate?

13. What question are you secretly glad I didn't ask you this week?

14. Do you find any women in your work circle, church, neighborhood or elsewhere especially attractive? Who are they? (Note: This question is appropriate only to answer with one other man who will keep the response in absolute confidence and hold you accountable.)

15. How have you longed for acclaim? Has ambition had its way in your life recently?

16. What roles have rationalization and denial played in your life recently? How do you keep a check on rationalization and denial?

17. Do your family friends and personal friends encourage you to act in ways that glorify God?

18. What have you done recently that gave you a sense of power?

19. What substances, if any, have you been abusing?

20. Where have you gone on the Internet lately that you're ashamed to admit?

21. What is one thing about yourself that you really don't want others to know about?

Write down any questions you want your accountability group or friend to regularly ask you.